SPIRITUAL Calculations

THE SECRETS TO PERFECTING THE RULES OF ROYALTY

DR. Y. BUR

Available Titles

ASITPLEASESGOD.COM

Spiritual Calculations

The Secrets to Perfecting the Rules of Royalty

Copyright © 2021 by Dr. Y. Bur. All rights reserved.

Visit www.RoarPublishingGroup.com for more information. No part of this publication may be reproduced, stored in a retrieval system, or transmitted in any way, electronic, mechanical, photocopy, recording, or otherwise, without the author's prior permission except as provided by USA copyright law.

Book design copyright © 2021 by R.O.A.R. International Group. All rights reserved.

R.O.A.R. Publishing Group
581 N. Park Ave. Ste. #725
Apopka, FL 32704
www.RoarPublishingGroup.com
DrY@DrYBur.com

Published in the United States of America
ISBN: 978-1-948936-49-1
$22.88

PLEASE SEND PRAYERS, TESTIMONIES, DONATIONS, OR ORDERS TO:

Dr. Y. Bur
R.O.A.R. Publishing Group
581 N. Park Ave. Ste. #725
Apopka, FL 32704
ROAR-58-2316
762-758-2316

Dr.YBur@gmail.com

Visit Us At:
AsItPleasesGodMovement
AsItPleasesGod

DrYBur.com
AsItPleasesGod.com

Please DONATE to this *Missionable Movement of God* as a GIVE-BACK to the Kingdom. Thanks for your support. Many Blessings.

AIPG Donation Link

Scan to Pay

Table of Contents

- INTRODUCTION ... 7
- CHAPTER 1 ... 11
  - Cross-Contamination ... 11
- CHAPTER 2 ... 21
  - Cross-Pollination ... 21
- CHAPTER 3 ... 33
  - Sacred Art ... 33
- CHAPTER 4 ... 43
  - Desert Experience ... 43
- CHAPTER 5 ... 55
  - Spiritual Amnesia ... 55
- CHAPTER 6 ... 63
  - Spiritual Baskets ... 63
- CHAPTER 7 ... 73
  - Spiritual Calculations ... 73
- CHAPTER 8 ... 81
  - Heavenly Manifold ... 81
- CHAPTER 9 ... 93
  - Heavenly Sprinkles ... 93
- CHAPTER 10 ... 105
  - Spiritual Dephasing ... 105

CHAPTER 11..	113
RULES OF ROYALTY..	113
CHAPTER 12..	155
DECLARATIONS OF REVELATION	155

Introduction

The truth about who we are is not a mystery, but we are a little fickle when it comes down to uncharted territory or the Kingdom of Heaven. The Elements of the Great Unknown, as well as the Mysteries of the Heavenly of Heavens, have been around since the beginning of time, whether we partake of science, nature, or anything in between. Frankly, they are well-calculated and are not going anywhere, regardless of our biased opinion or worldly nature. Therefore, we must step up to the plate at some point in our lives, seeking and doing more. More of what? It is more for WHOM! More for the Kingdom of Heaven as it relates to what we have or do not, more of what we understand or do not, and more of what we are privileged to obtain from a Spiritual Perspective or what we cannot.

The *Spiritual Calculations* of God contain boundaries we may or may not be privileged to have or understand. Unbeknown to most, our significance does not lie in people; it lies within us! Once we understand this fact, then it is relayed outwardly to impact the lives of others through our Purpose, Gifting, Calling, or Talents without condemning, shaming, or outing others. What is the purpose of doing so? We are the Spiritual Vessels God uses to accomplish His Divine Mission. If we do not understand ourselves, we will have difficulty understanding others, their story, or their reasoning. As a result, we will have several aborted self-engaged missions, thwarting the Impact or Image of God. Even if we have the heart to do the right thing, the wrong thing may come out, especially if we do not do a checkup from the neck up.

We all have a desire to belong to something or someone, giving us a feeling of security, love, comfort, and oneness. If we are stripped of any one of these desires, we will suffer some form of longing from within by Divine default. Yet, amid the longings, we must know what to do and how. If not, the gap becomes bigger, separating us from God, ourselves, and the ones we love, or we will begin seeking from others what we are unwilling to give or do for ourselves. In the carnality of it all, it will cause us to pick up negative habits to coax the unresolved perceptional feelings of our real or imagined deprivation. By far, our lack of understanding in this area leads to negative attributes such as discontentment, disobedience, rebellion, and confusion, causing us to become misunderstood, shunned, or judged based on our beliefs, habits, conditioning, attitude, and so on.

Everyone has a story, and with our story, we must understand and come to terms with it. Without understanding or owning our truth, we become susceptible to the worldliness of our choosing to coax the hidden pain, trauma, or atrocities we have been secretly or openly dealt. Even if we do not want to own our truth, talk about it, or choose to avoid it outright, the truth is that it does not go away. It becomes merely compounded with transferable rights into our Bloodline. However, all is not lost. With this book, there is HOPE.

Unbeknown to most, our life-changing experience is already *Spiritually Calculated* on the *Tablet of our Heart*. Now, in the process of living life, we must become willing to allow the *Spiritual Computing* process to take place, giving us a better understanding of our '*Why*.' With this understanding, we are better able to release the '*How To*' process to God without us having to make excuses, justify, or rationalize His Divine Timing to prove His Favor to others.

Once we eliminate the feeble excuses we present to ourselves, we are better able to take possession of the opportunity and positioning process to move at the Tune of God, not man. In most cases, if we are not adequately synced with the Spirit's Leading, we may miss the mark, even if we have the desire to do well. So, we must become Spiritually Unveiled to ensure we do not miss our cue while understanding that our Miracles, Blessings, and Anointing are already. Why do we need to know this? If we do not, the enemy can toss us to and fro due to our doubtfulness, while justifiably zapping our faith. How is this justified? There are a few ways, but not limited to such:

- [ ] If we do not learn how to contend with the Word of God, putting on the Whole Armor of God, zapping is justified.
- [ ] If we do not cancel negatives, replacing or counteracting them with positives, zapping is justified.
- [ ] If we operate in worldliness without repentance, zapping is justified.
- [ ] If we do not use the Fruits of the Spirit in our interactions with God, ourselves, and others, zapping is justified.
- [ ] If we are ungrateful, selfish, unruly, disobedient, or disrespectful, zapping is justified.
- [ ] If we are envious, jealous, cruel, hateful, evil, or covetous, zapping is justified.
- [ ] If we speak doom and gloom, levying curses over the lives of others, zapping is justified.
- [ ] If we are unforgiving or unmerciful, zapping is justified.
- [ ] If we are judgmental or holier than thou, degrading, demoralizing, or destroying the innocent, zapping is justified.
- [ ] If we cannot set a guard over our minds, tongues, and emotions, zapping is justified.
- [ ] If we refuse to help others out of selfishness, greed, envy, or pride, especially if it is within our power to do so, zapping is justified.
- [ ] If we defame, misuse, or manipulate the Word of God for selfish reasons or to bully, zapping is justified.

What is zapping from a Spiritual Perspective? It is the sifting process we will go through from the inside out with negativity, confusion, setbacks, failures, rejection, etc., which seems to come out of nowhere. But yet, in all reality, we have unawaringly left an open door without knowing how to close it properly.

Just so we are clear, I do not wish the zapping of the enemy upon anyone. I am ordained to bring forth the Divine Awareness needed to prevent one from suffering in such a manner without realizing what is taking place. More importantly, we need to know that no one is exempt from being negatively targeted. The zapping of the enemy is not just for us; it could linger in our Bloodline as well, especially if it is unrepentant, overlooked, whitewashed, fumbled, or we become dumbfounded by the ways of the enemy. For this reason, we need to become cautious about appearing right in our own eyes, taking a second look at our method of operation from God's Divine Perspective.

Why must we get His Perspective on things? Once again, our Blessings are already. Nevertheless, in the waiting process, it is our time of preparation, planning, positioning, and exhibiting proactiveness in what we are doing, saying, and becoming. According to the Heavenly of Heavens, it is not a time of playing around, parleying, pretending, or provoking the Hand of God to please ourselves selfishly.

In the Eye of God, everything is Divinely Calculated, and to move forward in the Spirit of Excellence, we need to know what to do and how to get it done the right way. In our selfless efforts, *As It Pleases God*, it is only wise to add Him to our equational efforts to Spiritually Download Divine Instructions. This book, *Spiritual Calculations*, provides the much-needed information on how to do so, *As It Pleases Him*, revealing the profound truth to truly excel in our endeavors.

This essential guide will empower you to invite God into your decision-making process, allowing you to download Spirit-Led instructions. Using this method, *As It Pleases Him*, ensures that your efforts are selfless and aligned with His Divine Will through the transformative insight of Divine Wisdom. So, if you are ready to flip the script on what is being zapped out of your equations, let us take this to the next level to avoid any form of *Cross-Contamination*.

Chapter 1

Cross-Contamination

The search for meaning is embedded in our DNA from the *Cross-Contamination* that took place in the Garden of Eden. Although we are clothed with access to our bare essentials such as oxygen, water, food, light, etc., God will not do all the work for us. Nor will He undo or uncross what we have crossed out of DISOBEDIENCE. According to the *Spiritual Calculations* from the Book of Genesis, we are required to do our share of labor and repent of our wrongdoings without passing the blame. If not, our Spiritual Hunger will become stronger with time instead of making life easier. Is this fair? Of course, it is. Contrary to what most may believe, this is a God-Ruled Nation. The moment we think we are above Him or we rule the World, we *Cross-Contaminate* our Bloodline with worldliness, setting certain character traits in motion by default.

In the ratherability of what we are discussing, according to the *Spiritual Calculations* from the Heavenly of Heavens, there is no such thing as a free ride in the Kingdom! From Genesis to Revelation, we tend not to appreciate the people, places, and things that do not cost us anything. So, we must put in the work, using the Spiritual, Navigational, or Relational Tools given to AWAKEN our Spirit Man. Respectfully speaking, if we choose not to work on ourselves from the inside out, we have no reason to blame anyone. Nor do we have the right to concoct superficial excuses for dropping the ball in any area, especially when it comes down to the utilization of our Gifts, Calling, or Talents.

Our relationship with God is of the utmost importance. We are created in His Image, and if we have a desire to receive the Spiritual Insight on how to perfect this image in ourselves, we must go to the Source. Nevertheless, with this sort of Spiritual Reliance comes responsibility. We cannot become careless or comfortable with our Blessings or Birthrights, thinking we do not need to maintain them. If we become pompous in such a manner, it will lead to some form of recklessness and ungodly *Cross-Contamination*. According to the *Spiritual Calculations* of the Heavenly of Heavens, to keep all God has for us requires us to become humble, faithful, diligent, obedient, grateful, and merciful.

If we want our Blessings to multiply, we cannot sit around twiddling our thumbs, hoping our inner change will come; we must become a work-in-progress, developing what is already within. If not, we will find ourselves looking for healing, hope, and restoration in others, resulting in constant disappointment. A Blessing can mean something different to each of us based on our current situation, circumstances, conditioning, or biases. Yet, whatever we seek begins from within the human psyche, spreading outwardly.

Suppose we seek whatever or whomever from the outside in. In this case, it creates backwardness in the Realm of the Spirit and the Eye of God. How is this possible? We are Spirit first. If we do not know or understand this fact, we can become our worst enemy without realizing it or outright turning on ourselves. Besides, it may also limit our ability to recognize our Blessings due to some form of Spiritual Blindness, Deafness, or Muteness. As a result, we will find ourselves seeking our Blessings in all the wrong places, with the wrong people, and through worldly means, overlooking the Heavenly Treasures hidden in the Inherited or Spoken Blessings of the Spirit.

Listen, nothing makes it into our physical realm without some form of Spiritual Development; therefore, if we go to the Source of our ailment, we are better able to pinpoint the *Cross-Contaminating* factors or our point of misdirection. Really? Yes, really! The Spirit knows all, providing liberation to those who become One with the Holy Spirit, revealing things the soul will opt to keep hidden. The soulish man wants to stay in charge by creating soul ties, bondages, and yokes to keep us on a leash while *Cross-Contaminating* our Bloodline with unrealized worldliness. If we think for a minute, our soul wants to relinquish its power, then think again. It will fight us unless we awaken our Spirit to become One with the Holy Spirit to tame our psyche and cover ourselves with the Blood of Jesus.

How do we recognize our connection to the Holy Spirit? The first sign is through humility. The second sign is when our conscience begins to guide, correct, or discipline us in the areas we would usually overlook or where we would typically not feel any form of guilt when indulging. Thirdly, it is when we begin to use the Fruits of the Spirit (Love, Joy, Peace, Patience, Kindness, Goodness, Faithfulness, Gentleness, and Self-Control) automatically, or when they come to mind as a reminder when we omit using them. By far, the *Spiritually Calculated* factors hidden in the Fruits of the Spirit create an active and proactive form of Spiritual Awareness, causing us to become or do better the next time around when falling short of our Heavenly Expectations.

Humility has been whitewashed in a way that our cover-up has outweighed our Spiritual Fruits. We have been conditioned to put on a show or develop masks to cover up the true person without correction. How is it possible to put on a show, especially when we are who we are? It is often recognized in our people skills, but it is not limited to such. For example, with the Fruits of the Spirit, listed below are a few ways we often whitewash them without realizing it:

- ☐ We exhibit Love in front of others, but behind closed doors, we behave like hellions on wheels, spewing hatefulness in our words, actions, deeds, thoughts, beliefs, and attitudes.

- ☐ We exhibit the illusion of Joy in public, but we do not have a clue that joy comes from within. At the same time, our hearts are oozing negativity all over the place, zapping the life out of others without any form of remorse.

- ☐ We exhibit Peace around those who do not know we are one step away from coming unglued behind closed doors with those we claim to love.

- ☐ We exhibit Patience with those we stand to gain from, yet we are impatient with those who have nothing to offer.

- ☐ We exhibit Kindness to those who support our likes, dislikes, or behaviors, but we are unkind to those who know or question our truth.

- ☐ We exhibit Goodness to those who provide a benefit and slap the hand or become evil to those who appear not to be useful to us or for us.

- ☐ We exhibit Faithfulness in the Holy of Holies, but behind closed doors, our wavering faith becomes evident in our inconsistencies and doubtfulness.

- ☐ We exhibit Gentleness to those who give us what we want, yet when our expectations are unmet, we become abrasive, rude, or disobedient.

- ☐ We exhibit Self-Control for a show, but our inner man is crying out with an unquenchable thirst that is secretly driving us insane.

Character development is crucial for the Kingdom. Suppose we do not develop ourselves in and out of the Spiritual Classroom. In this case, we may get caught up Mentally, Physically, Emotionally, or Spiritually with people, places, and things catering to our weaknesses, longings, or deprivation. What does this mean? We are only as strong as our weakest link. If we do not know what it is, then rest assured, it will be the place the enemy will attack, sideswipe, derail, or provoke us.

For this reason, we need to become loyal to ourselves, owning our truth. By doing so, if we are called out on our folly for whatever reason or however, we will not get upset, angry, or become unglued. Instead, we can own our weaknesses, repent, and keep it moving with outright humility.

Now, on the other side of humility, if we think we are doing great things, destroying the innocent, tearing down the Kingdom of God, or outright exhibiting hatefulness, we must exercise extreme caution. This sort of behavior is frowned upon because innocent bystanders can get hurt amid our pompous escapades. For this reason, we must understand a few things, but not limited to such:

- ☐ Our Blessings may not be from God, so we must check the Source. Then again, we also need to pinpoint the secret or open rendering of our sacrifice or idolatrous efforts.
- ☐ God is using our Blessings to make us Believers.
- ☐ He is allowing our 'COME UP' to BLESS another for His Purpose.
- ☐ God is using us as a footstool to transfer wealth.
- ☐ He is using our greed or negative *Cross-Contamination* to annihilate our Bloodline.
- ☐ God is using us to train another for the Kingdom.
- ☐ He is opening or closing our Spiritual Eyes, Ears, or Mouth.
- ☐ God is making our waywardness a Blessing or Miracle for another.
- ☐ He is using us to reposition, regraft, or reconcile another.
- ☐ God is proving He is above all of our idols or little gods.
- ☐ He is transferring our Spiritual Mantle or Birthright to another.
- ☐ God is *Spiritually Calculating* our demise, making an example out of us to promote the Kingdom of Heaven.

If we are deceived into believing worldliness is the way to the Kingdom's Treasures, we can abort the Spiritual Mission or transfer our Spiritual Rights. How is this possible when our

Blessings are already? We cannot tempt God with our agenda or take our Spiritual Privileges for granted. When we do not feel Blessed or when we are not being a Blessing, we become DESPERATE. Regardless of what we believe or how we feel, Spiritual Transfers and Annulments of Birthrights are real, similar to how Esau sold his Birthrights to Jacob for a meal in Genesis 25.

The bottom line is that Esau lacked the value needed to take possession of his Birthright at the appropriate time, whereas Jacob saw the value and would do anything to get it.

For the most part, Jacob lacked faith in his Birthright or Blessing. Based upon this hidden insecurity, he felt justified in manipulating and outright tricking God, his father, and his twin brother by becoming someone whom he was not, only to feel Blessed or create a Blessed Illusion. Was this right? Absolutely not! First and foremost, we cannot trick God, and *Spiritually Calculating* against God is outright foolery to the Kingdom, causing us to become the joke in due time.

Secondly, his trickster mother did not make the situation better; she divided her house, *Cross-Contaminating* the Bloodline with her bare hands, pitting one brother against another. How is this possible? Obviously, each child became accustomed to having their way with their favored parent. As a result, Esau took foreign wives at his discretion out of rebellion and disobedience, *Cross-Contaminating* the Bloodline without the discretion of God, his father, or his mother. We cannot say he did not know; he knew!

As a privileged child, Esau did not care about his behavior or actions as long as his favor got him what he wanted when he wanted it. As a result of Esau's hot-headed, ill-mannered, disobedient, and egotistical demeanor, it helped to seal the secret animosity for his mother. How? She manipulated her favorite son, Jacob, into stealing the Birthright that Esau sold for a right-now meal.

In my opinion, if Rebekah had prepared them to embrace their BLESSINGS as opposed to showing favoritism, Esau and Jacob would have embraced their individuality. Plus, they would not have been coveting each other or outright exhibiting the negative characteristics of jealousy, envy, and disrespect in the camp or their house. Truthfully, without a doubt, the partially instigated sibling rivalry could have been brought to a halt. How? If one parent had stepped up to the plate to build value in respecting the differences in one another, squashing the elements of selfishness and favoritism, it would have changed the trajectory by default.

Although there is no 100% perfect family, we can master the power of communication to effectively relate to each other without having to engage in underhanded behaviors, selfishness, or feelings of unworthiness due to some form of favoritism.

As a result of this sort of Spiritual Negligence on behalf of all involved, when the time came in Genesis 27 for the transference of Birthrights, Jacob received what his brother took for granted. Although Esau had the audacity to get upset, wanting to kill his brother, Jacob still paid a hefty price for partaking in the process of deception. How so? The price for his deception mimicked the feeling of death from the inside out. Unfortunately, it is a gut-wrenching feeling to have our conscience eat at us, reminding us of our deceptive folly.

Why would Jacob pay the price for what God allowed to happen? He had to wrestle with God regarding his inner demons of deception, tainting his Bloodline. What was the price? Listed below are a few penalties, but not limited to such:

- ☐ He lost the trust of his father.
- ☐ He lost the strained brotherly bond of Esau.
- ☐ He lost the covering and favoritism of his mother.
- ☐ He lost the communion of family.
- ☐ He was forced to live alone in an unknown land.
- ☐ He was deceived by and enslaved for the woman he loved most.
- ☐ He was deceived into marrying a woman he did not love to become fruitful.
- ☐ His sons became deceitful, manipulative, and scheming with the Principles and the Word of God.

- ☐ He lost the woman he truly loved in childbirth with her second child, who stole household idols from her father and lied about it.
- ☐ His daughter was tricked and raped.
- ☐ His children betrayed him repeatedly, eventually selling Joseph, his favorite son, into slavery.
- ☐ He had to wrestle with his inner demons of betrayal continually.

In the totality of it all, before God commissioned Jacob in pursuit of the Promise, He had to drive the trickster out of him. More importantly, his behavior did not exempt his Bloodline from experiencing the consequences and repercussions of trickery; instead, it created a domino effect.

Let this be a lesson for us all; we must account for the *Spiritual Calculations* of our behaviors to ensure we do not curse or *Cross-Contaminate* our Bloodline. In the same way we *Cross-Contaminate*, we can also *Uncross the Contamination* to create endless possibilities, *As It Pleases God*. How? In Genesis 32, the same way Jacob wrestled with God face-to-face to break the generational strongholds, we have the same power as well.

Most of us think Jacob wrestled for himself, but I beg to differ. He wrestled for his Bloodline. He had enough of the trickster mentality clouding his future. And with this heartfelt decision, he was not willing to let go until God blessed him, removing the yoke of bondage or *Cross-Contamination* stemming from his past. As a result, God directly and indirectly preserved his Bloodline, changing his name Jacob 'Trickster' to Israel and separating the old from the new. More importantly, we are still capitalizing on the Blessings of him, *Uncrossing the Contamination*.

What can we do to *Uncross Contaminants* of our own making? We must begin to *Cross-Pollinate* with Seeds of Goodness, Uprightness, and Integrity. How do we go about doing so? Listed below are a few items, but not limited to such:

- ☐ Place God first in all things, involving Him in all of our decisions.
- ☐ Assume responsibility for ourselves, thoughts, behaviors, reactions, and beliefs.
- ☐ Exhibit the Fruits of the Spirit in all we do, say, and become.
- ☐ Counteract negatives with positive affirmations or the Word of God.
- ☐ Focus on communicating effectively with equal and fair treatment.
- ☐ Refrain from judging, criticizing, or whitewashing.
- ☐ Avoid negative categorizing, name-calling, belittling, or stereotyping due to our secret or open biases.
- ☐ Master creating a win-win regardless of how it may appear.
- ☐ Focus on doing well with clean hands and a pure heart.
- ☐ Forgive ourselves and others, becoming compassionate and merciful with no strings attached.
- ☐ Be willing to step into the Spiritual Classroom at the drop of a dime while continuously checking our motives for selfishness, pompousness, or favoritism.
- ☐ Focus on sharing and Blessing others as a Servant of the Kingdom of Heaven.

Cross-Pollination is not often associated with the Elements of the Spirit, yet it is so powerful in the Kingdom of Heaven. Keep in mind that no one is perfect; therefore, if one falls short, repent, regraft, or uproot while keeping it moving toward Kingdom Righteousness. Why does this happen to us as Believers? Distractions will come to get us off track. We need to know what to do and when to prevent any form of negative festers from popping up or taking root, Mentally, Physically, Emotionally, and Spiritually.

The positive, productive, and fruitful work-in-progress mentality keeps us from negatively wallowing, ensuring we become better and not bitter. Better yet, it also enhances the *Pollination* Process to prevent ourselves or our Bloodline from becoming a follynation (a nation full of folly) in the Eye of God. The truth of the matter is, according to the *Spiritual Calculations* of the Heavenly of Heavens, we are the Gift that keeps on Giving. If we believe in ourselves, our Birthright, and our Legacy, focusing on learning, doing, and becoming more in the Kingdom with a Positive Mindset, we can change the trajectory of our lives, especially if we become obedient to the Leading of the Lord.

In concordance with the Kingdom's Revelation to all, it makes us proactively effective when operating in the Spirit of Excellence. However, when we incorporate God into the equation to create a win-win out of everything, it makes our Spiritual Pollen positively potent. Once we understand the *Rules of Royalty* and gain our Kingdom Credentials, there is nothing we cannot achieve according to the Will of God. So, if one is ready, let us go deeper.

Chapter 2

Cross-Pollination

When we think about pollen, we have been conditioned to associate it with powdery, dusty, or fine microspores with adverse factors, causing or triggering allergies, spreading sicknesses, and transporting diseases. All of these factors are true, acting as a curse for some, whereas pollen is considered a Divine Blessing from a Spiritual Perspective. Yet somehow, we do not see it as such due to the seeming inconveniences it may cause to those falling victim. Thus, it serves its purpose with or without our permission for the trees, grass, weeds, and flowers. Amazing as it is, its goal is to preserve and fertilize its Bloodline, creating a life form for our benefit in some way while contributing to the Cycle of Life.

How does this information about pollen benefit us as Believers? It does its part as it relates to its Divine Mission, irrespective of what we think, say, feel, or do. From my perspective, if we could somehow develop this same mindset when it comes down to the Spiritual Fertilization of the human protégé, we can *Cross-Pollinate* on a Spiritual Level, putting our enemies at bay, or putting them to boot, at any time, on any day of the week, period.

In and out of the Cycles of Life, if we ignore nature or its method of operation, we will sometimes miss out on the natural process of Divine Design or Life Cycles, causing a form of disrespect without us realizing it. How would disrespect come into play here? Everything has been designed to heal itself, reproducing after its own kind, and if we get upset with pollen being on our car, then who has the problem? The problem is from within us, not within the pollen, right? Absolutely!

The pollen did its job to point out our weakness, yet we failed to take heed to the simple lesson hidden in the pollen. How is this possible, especially when we have dominion? First, the pollen was following its Divine Design of transportation. Secondly, God has granted us the ability to have a running car to get us from point A to point B without us having to walk. More importantly, according to the Cycle of Life, our means of transportation hinder the pollen's conveyance process. Thirdly, He has also given us running water to freely rinse the pollen off, thus helping the pollen find its way to the soil because our humanly vehicles of convenience hinder its natural process.

If we have the nerve to get upset about the pollination process or any Cycle of Nature, then we have work to do in the Spiritual Classroom. Why do we need a little work due to disagreeing with nature? According to the *Spiritual Calculations* hidden from within, our human nature is getting in the way of our Spiritual Nature. How do we make this make sense? Once again, it is through the hidden Elements of Respect. For example, if we disrespect Mother Nature, She will find a way to prove a point to us, with or without our permission. Is this real? Of course, it is. Even if we do not believe in Mother Nature, Her DNA is indeed flowing through us; thus, if we disrespect Her, it only indicates a lack of respect from within the human psyche.

Furthermore, if one has not noticed by now, regardless of the use of proper grammar or the judgments of others, I write with Spiritual Respect. Although I break the man-made grammar rules, I do not break the Spiritual Rules of Respect. As it relates to my Spiritual Calling and Anointing, personally, I cannot glean from the Heavenly of Heavens on this Spiritual Level without exhibiting Spiritual Respect, period!

Now, in the *Cross-Pollination* process, if we do not develop the Elements of Respect, we will find people developing a deaf ear to us due to our method of operation, character, or the violation of the free will of others. In this process, we cannot become control freaks; it dilutes our effectiveness to freely fertilize or selflessly share with no strings attached.

Just so we are clear, the *'no strings attached'* does not mean *'something for nothing'* or the *'something for something'* mentality; it is the *'In Purpose on purpose'* demeanor. What type of demeanor is this? It is the ability to redirect our point of focus on Heavenly Treasures to ensure we do not become caught up in materialism or fake facades to prove our worthiness.

Listen, we are all here for a reason, having a specific job to do for the Kingdom. If we are not fulfilling it, selfishness can easily set in, crippling our Divine Mission, especially if we are not careful. How can we pinpoint whether we are in Purpose on purpose? We must ask ourselves fact-finding questions, such as, but not limited to:

☐ Are we doing this for the Kingdom, or are we doing this for ourselves?

☐ Are we sharing love in this endeavor, or are we spreading corruption and hate?

☐ Are we casting doom and gloom, or are we building others?

☐ Are we exhibiting the Fruits of the Spirit, or are we sharing rotten fruits to spoil the fruits of others?

☐ Are we exhibiting Christlike Character, or are we playing by our own rules?

☐ Are we in control of our tongue, or are we playing Russian roulette with it?

☐ Are we governing our thoughts positively, or are we allowing our thoughts to run wild with negativity?

- ☐ Are we allowing our soulish ways to rule us, or are we allowing the Holy Spirit to govern our Mind, Body, Soul, and Spirit?

- ☐ Are we exhibiting selfishness, or are we exhibiting unselfish behaviors?

- ☐ Are we striving to use or suck the life out of others, or are we being an asset or bringing life to others?

- ☐ Are we always on the take (the what can I get out of it) mode, or are we always in the sharing or giving mode?

- ☐ Are we allowing ourselves to bully others, or are we allowing ourselves to positively impact the lives of others and the Kingdom of Heaven?

We cannot take the simple things in life for granted because they may hold a powerful secret or reasoning we can glean from to revolutionize our lives beyond human comprehension. Amazingly, this is why the Bible refers to ants as a paralleled or colonized reference to what He is seeking from us. Yet, we look at an ant as a small, invaluable insect when it has the Spiritual Principles to *Cross-Pollinate* our lives for generations to come. How is this possible if we have dominion over them? Just because we have dominion does not mean we use it correctly or as God intended. How do we not use it correctly as Believers? We have interjected worldly and selfish means into the Kingdom, thinking we have Heavenly Dominion when we do not. God is the Ruler of it all, regardless of what we are conditioned to believe.

Now, just so we are clear, we can receive Heaven on Earth Dominion, but this must be earned through a Spiritual Alliance, *As It Pleases God*. We must have the Father, Son, and Holy Spirit as the Trinity leading the way. We cannot have one foot in the Kingdom and one foot out, playing around with God or His Spiritual Protocols. Spiritually, this is a quick way to get put 6-feet under, die a slow death from the inside out, or wipe out or possibly curse our Bloodline, even if we have made the sacrifice to go to the dark side to get some form of access, riches, or privileges. In my opinion, it is best to approach the Kingdom the right way to avoid the unnecessary backlash of Spiritual Correction.

How can we develop a Kingdom Mentality from ants? First and foremost, they respect their queen, allowing her to reproduce after their own kind. Secondly, they delegate individuals to take care, nurture, develop, and train their offspring without them deviating from their designated role. Thirdly, they have the workers who build, rebuild, and do whatever it takes to keep their homes in order, even when humans intentionally crush their mounds. Fourthly, they have soldiers protecting their mound from invaders, and they will not back down in defending their queen.

According to the *Spiritual Calculations* of Time, for decades, ants have outnumbered and outsmarted humans, but we are often in denial. Why are we in denial? Because we are able to build, create, and maneuver on a level that an ant cannot. But when it comes down to our Spiritual Senses, we are defeated. How is this possible?

- ☐ Ants have more than 12,000 species, while proactively multiplying rapidly in secret. In my opinion, they do not play around with their offspring; it is said that one queen can have millions of babies in a span of a few years. We have put a cap on the '*Be fruitful and multiply and replenish the earth*' decree to ensure we can afford a certain lifestyle with freedom. By far, this is indeed our God-Given right, so we cannot blame the ants for becoming a million to one of us. The million-to-one ratio proves we need to pay attention to their ways, as the Bible speaks about in the Book of Proverbs.

- ☐ Ants can destroy anything man-made with time because they are masters of the dirt. They know that with time, the power hidden in the elements of dirt can reduce, infect, or cause dysfunction in anything man-made.

☐ Ants protect their legacy by hiding and safeguarding the queen with their lives. But more importantly, ants have become wiser for their sake by having more than one queen in the colony. As we all know, we cannot overcome a colony of ants unless we take out the queen or queens, and then, with time, the colony will die off. In my opinion, they have outsmarted insecticides by *Cross-Pollinating* and creating satellite nests to distract what they perceive as intruders, even if they are doing the intruding.

☐ Ants do not possess ears, but they are not deaf; yet, they use their senses to hear through vibrations. They do not have lungs, but they breathe oxygen through other parts of their body. In my opinion, they use what they have to get what they want, even if it means slave-raiding other colonies to build their labor force to survive.

☐ Ants do not give up easily, settle for defeat, make excuses, or become emotional—they find a way to accomplish their mission by any means necessary.

☐ Ants leave a trail of pheromones to track their journey, find their way back, communicate with other ants, and send warnings of impending danger, leaving a legacy of wisdom that will outlast them without having the ability to read, write, speak, or articulate.

☐ Ants are everywhere; they have *Cross-Pollinated* to all corners of the globe except for one place bearing a part of their name, *Ant*arctica. Not bad for an ant whose brain is like a grain of salt to ours and is considered to be the smartest insect according to the Bible. How is this possible? An ant's brain operates as a colony and not as an individual brain, as we are accustomed to functioning. Plus, we have too much tit-for-tat selfishness, jealousy, pride, envy, and coveting, plaguing and dividing our Kingdom's maneuverability, zapping our creativity and ONENESS.

☐ Ants pride themselves on being socially capitalistic, using every opportunity to build their colony by working as a team. In a colony, teamwork is essential to the proper functioning of its method of operation.

☐ Ants are very witty, sneaky, and aggressive when they want to let us know we have offended them. How is this possible? When an ant bites us, do we feel the crawl or the bite first? When an ant damages our property, do we see the damage before the ant? Most often, the damage has already taken place before the ants or the infestation becomes noticeable.

☐ Ants evolve or adapt similarly to humans, striving to overcome and abound, creating a win-win for the sake of their colonized efforts.

☐ Ants are effective in their ability to share. Although very small, they possess two stomachs—one for themselves and one to share with others who have other duties to the colony or queen.

☐ Ants do not attempt to become anything other than their Divine Design, doing what ants do best. What do they do best? Tilling the soil, *Cross-Pollinating*, providing for their colony in a certain capacity, taking back what they feel belongs to them, and replenishing the earth. At the same time, it is one of the best success stories of Spiritual Discipline and Diligence in the Eye of God.

What is the big deal about ants, right? According to scripture, this is what it tells us: *"Go to the ant, you sluggard! Consider her ways and be wise, which, having no captain, overseer, or ruler, provides her supplies in the summer, and gathers her food in the harvest. How long will you slumber, O sluggard? When will you rise from your sleep? A little sleep, a little slumber, a little folding of the hands to sleep—so shall your poverty come on you like a prowler, and your need like an armed man."* Proverbs 6:6-11.

Ants have outlived most animals, but when it is all said and done, they feel as if we are the intruders, and we feel as if they are as well. Based upon years of study, if we dare to take note and use their Colonized Principles in addition to our Spiritual Ones, we can revamp the real meaning of who we are from the inside out. If we take a look at the word servant, we will also see the word 'ANT' hidden at the end of the word servANT. Therefore, if we proactively and diligently serve the Kingdom of Heaven as a little ant, we will be able to shake Heaven and Earth. When this Symbolic Fertilizer of Servanthood is appropriately used in conjunction with our Spiritual Covenant, we will also find the word 'ANT' in the word covenANT. Is this a coincidence? Absolutely not!

The Bible is riddled with the words 'Servant' and 'Covenant,' which are both used in agreement with God's Promises. Unbeknown to most, these two words can create a serious *Cross-Pollination* of Greatness according to the *Spiritual Calculations* of the Heavenly of Heavens.

If we use the Fruits of the Spirit to SEAL our Oneness to the Covenant of God as a willing and obedient Spiritual Servant to the Kingdom while having clean hands and a pure heart, our name will become written in the Book of Life. Is this Biblical? Absolutely! It says, *"In the middle of its street, and on either side of the river, was the tree of life, which bore twelve fruits, each tree yielding its fruit every month. The leaves of the tree were for the healing of the nations. And there shall be no more curse, but the Throne of God and of the Lamb shall be in it, and His <u>servants</u> shall serve Him. They shall see His face, and His name shall be on their foreheads. There shall be no night there: They need no lamp nor light of the sun, for the Lord God gives them light. And they shall reign forever and ever."* Revelation 22:2-5.

"Behold, I am coming quickly! Blessed is he who keeps the words of the prophecy of this book." Revelation 22:7.

Now, on the other hand, if we become so uppity or pompous, negating the ability to unselfishly serve others or downplaying our Spiritual Covenantal responsibilities, we will find that God will allow us, the ones we love, or our Bloodline to succumb to the issues of life. What does this mean? We are given over to our own lust to become the other type of *Captive Slave Ant* called merchANT or inhabitANT, according to the Book of Revelation. What is the difference?

☐ The Merchants are caught up in buying, selling, merchandising, materialism, and hustling due to some form of greed, jealousy, envy, or covetousness. Is this Biblical? *"For all the nations have drunk of the wine of the wrath of her fornication, the kings of the earth have committed fornication with her, and the <u>merchants</u> of the earth have become rich through the abundance of her luxury. And I heard another voice from heaven saying, Come out of her, my people, lest you share in her sins, and lest you receive of her plagues."* Revelation 18:3-4. *"And the <u>merchants</u> of the earth will weep and mourn over her, for no one buys their merchandise anymore."* Revelation 18:11.

☐ The Inhabitants are those who diligently take up space, serving their own purpose and getting caught up in negative habits or their own ways of doing things without having God in the picture. Is this Biblical? Yes, it is. I love people too much, and I am so merciful; therefore, I could not make this up, even if I tried. Nevertheless, here is what it says, *"Then one of the seven angels who had the seven bowls came and talked with me, saying to me, Come, I will show you the judgment of the great harlot who sits on many waters, with whom the kings of the earth committed fornication, and the <u>inhabitants</u> of the earth were made drunk with the wine of her fornication."* Revelation 17:1-2.

If we are caught up in what is presently trending, beware! Why must we exercise extreme caution as Believers? It was the merchants who turned the House of the Lord into a place of mockery. Matthew 21:12-13 says, *"Then Jesus went into the Temple of God and drove out all those who bought and sold in the Temple, and overturned the tables of the money changers and the seats of those who sold doves. And He said to them, 'It is written, My house shall be called a House of Prayer, but you have made it a den of thieves.' "*

Regardless of how we make our income, God weighs the intents of our hearts. For example, Rahab was a harlot according to the Word of God; yet, based upon the contents of her heart, her Servanthood, and her Covenantal Awareness as it relates to the Children of Israel, it changed her story. She possessed a few character traits, causing her virtue to stand out in the Eye of God. For example, the character traits were wrapped in her sacrifice of:

- ☐ Kindliness.
- ☐ Friendliness.
- ☐ Trustworthiness.
- ☐ Faithfulness.
- ☐ Mercifulness.
- ☐ Helpfulness.
- ☐ Patience.
- ☐ Hospitability.
- ☐ Repentfulness.
- ☐ Wisdom.
- ☐ Usability.
- ☐ Willingness.

It does not matter where we are in life or who we are; our character is of the utmost importance in the Kingdom. Why must we work on our character traits, *As It Pleases God*? First, we all have a little hidden shadiness in us based on the Spiritual Law of Duality, knowing good and evil, with equals and opposites. Secondly, our occupation does not determine our character; we do! Thirdly, we must stop judging others to determine their worthiness.

Do we not have the free will to judge? Yes, we have free will to do whatever with whomever we like. But let me say this: The *Spiritual Calculations* of God cannot be matched or determined by us, period. Frankly, He will use anyone or anything to accomplish His Divine Mission, regardless of what we think, say, or attempt to circumvent. More importantly, what we see as worthy on the outside looking in with our human perspectives may not be what God views as worthiness from the inside out.

Nevertheless, by Rahab's unselfish decision to help the spies on God's behalf, she was *Cross-Pollinated* to receive a Great Reward. He allowed her to marry into the Tribe of Judah through Salmon, one of the spies, and then become the mother of Boaz. With this lineage, it placed Rahab as the great-great-grandmother of King David. Yes, we all know about David, right? The young shepherd boy, the one who slayed the other type of *Challenge Ant*, called the GiANT, which Spiritually Sealed his place as King.

Before we end this chapter, just as Rahab was *Spiritually Sealed* into the Lineage of Jesus, so are we, according to the *Spiritual Calculations* of the Heavenly of Heavens. We are all sisters and brothers in Christ Jesus. Just keep in mind, in or out of the Kingdom, Rahab wants us to know that our Blessings are usually hidden behind the GiANT in need of slaying, Mentally, Physically, Emotionally, and Spiritually, to leave our Mark or to obtain the Mark until the end of time.

Plus, regardless of the labels we placed on Rahab, she saved her Bloodline, allowing us to become covered by the Blood of Jesus through her simple acts of obedience. Now the question is, 'How about you?' 'Are you saving or destroying your Bloodline?' 'Is what you are doing today going to outlive you?'

By understanding the power hidden in a Covenantal Relationship with God, we can jump on board as Servants to do our part in the Kingdom, *As It Pleases Him*. Everything we need is already *Spiritually Calculated* in Spirit Form, so slaying the stereotypical

GiANTS in such a manner can invoke the *Sacred Art* from within to come forth.

Chapter 3

Sacred Art

In God weighing our hearts and the *Spiritual Calculations* of the Heavenly of Heavens, we are responsible for enhancing and developing the Kingdom through learning, understanding, sharing, and teaching. To do so, we must practice before we can perfect this *Sacred Art*. What is *Sacred Art*? Our Sacred Meaning, Birthright, Purpose, Gifting, or our 'Why' in life that we become ACTIVELY involved in. The moment we refuse to involve ourselves in Kingdom Mentorship or Mantleship, we will find ourselves amid secularism, jumping from one thing or one person to the next with little or no consistency, stability, or staying power.

By far, from a Spiritual Perspective, it is not wise to think we can skip grades in the Elements of God or His Sacredness. Unfortunately, *Sacred Art* does not operate in this manner; as a matter of fact, it will cause us to fall into a cycle of déjà vu as opposed to delivering us. Now, if we have become so self-aggrandizing, taking shortcuts or the easy way out, we may miss out on the vital lessons needed to protect and correct ourselves, or what would make a radical difference in our lives and with others.

As a Spiritual Artist by Divine Design, we must also understand that there are hidden Gifts, Talents, and Creativity in everyone in need of being extracted. We must find a way to convey this message with the Fruits of the Spirit, making the acceptance palatable to those who may have secretly lost hope or faith in the Kingdom. Deception is all around us and sometimes within us, without us realizing it, due to our known or unknown conditioning or worldliness. Truthfully, most often, due to our perceptions, expectations, or biases, we create most of our deception on our own. For this reason, we must weigh our motives with the Fruits of the Spirit. What is the purpose of doing so? They are the correctional or examining tools used in mastering our *Sacred Art* from within. From a Spiritual Perspective, this is why we should not attempt to cheat the Spiritual Classroom of the vital lessons we need for the Kingdom. If we miss the Spiritual Lessons, we may miss the message or our cue while interjecting our agenda instead of submitting to God's.

Here is the deal: If we begin to learn how to have a God-to-self, self-to-self, and person-to-person relationship of authentic transparency, we can break the yoke of selfishness. In addition, it will also provide a Spiritual Safety Net to remove the masks of pretense, giving us the confidence needed to move forward with no regrets. More importantly, it also gives us Spiritual Disclosure of the *Sacred Art* of God that most are not privy to, due to some form of blindness, deafness, or muteness. If we do not learn how to dialogue effectively in a Christlike manner, setting a guard over our tongues, our Spiritual Awareness can become thwarted. What does this mean? Sadly, this is when we confuse the Acts of God with the enemy's deception, talking ourselves and others out of their Blessings, similar to the deception in the Garden of Eden with Adam and Eve.

According to the *Spiritual Calculations* from the Heavenly of Heavens, it is always best to assume responsibility for our erring process. It helps us to remain transparent to our open or hidden truths, helping to master our ability to become and remain humble with a work-in-progress mentality. Sacredness requires peace and humility. If we are warring within our souls, we can get mixed feelings or become too temperamental, reflecting signs of an empty vessel as opposed to being filled with the Holy Spirit in an Earthen Vessel. What is the difference? Frankly, it is a matter of Self-Control or the lack of it. Now, suppose we involve the Fruits of the Spirit and the Holy Trinity (The Father, Son, and Holy Spirit) in our lives to become active participants. In this case, it helps to develop us into a *Sacred Vessel* in due season.

Just so we are clear, our *Sacredness* is not an overnight process. Why not? Are we not instantly perfected as Believers? No, we are not. We have layers of debris, hurt, trauma, conditioning, and biases in need of purging. Although the imparting, revelation, salvation, and availability of the Holy Trinity are immediate, the Kingdom Mentality is developed.

If we do not go through the Kingdom's Developmental Phase, *As It Pleases God*, we will attempt to operate in the Kingdom with a slave mentality of judgment, bondage, and rod irons. When operating in this manner, we will consciously or unconsciously circumvent God's Divine Mission with our own narratives. Spiritually, this is similar to God bringing the Children of Israel out of Egypt while taking them 40 years of wandering in the desert to get Egypt out of them. Picturesquely, can one imagine running the Kingdom of God like we run our own houses when no one is looking? I digress with this question, let us move on...

The Sacredness of God will NOT reside if we do not ABIDE in His Divine Will and Ways, *As It Pleases Him*. Choosing to behave like a disrespectful hellion on wheels without any form of repentance or correction will definitely cause us to get a side-eye from Him.

What makes *Sacredness* so crucial in the Eye of God? Our Christlike Character is linked to our Divine Sacredness, regardless of how we behave in public and behind closed doors.

We often do not discuss *Sacredness* due to the lack of understanding of its fine *Art*. Why do we avoid talking about *Sacredness*? Most often, we do not understand it. So we avoid it or use the camouflage of purity (cleanliness) to whitewash *Sacredness*. In the Eye of God, cleanliness and Holiness are not the same, nor should we avoid the discussion of both to develop the *Art of Purity*.

The *Art of Purity* is often frowned upon and rejected by those who are caught up in people, places, and things while sugarcoating the lust of the eyes, the lust of the flesh, and the pride of life. Of course, no one is exempt from these lusts, but they must be dealt with accordingly to keep our *Sacredness* top-notch.

What makes *Sacredness* so special in the Eye of God? Our *Divine Sacredness* is predicated on genuine transparency, repentance, humility, and the quality of character, *As It Pleases Him*. Conversely, worldly sacredness is predicated on unholy things, objects, or idols due to selfishness, pride, greed, or a desire to become a demigod. If we decide to pursue our *Sacred Art* outside of the Kingdom in a whole bunch of debauchery or evil practices, we are only deceiving ourselves into thinking peace will reside within us. In the Eye of God, it is only an illusion, causing us to create superficial masks.

Sacredness, according to the Kingdom, is considered Holiness. We cannot entertain certain people, places, and things that have the potential to zap our power, provoke a weakness, or reopen wounds of trauma. Now, if we choose to go about doing our own thing or the wrong thing out of disobedience, we can lose our covering due to Spiritual Negligence. For this reason, Matthew 7:6 warns, "*Do not give what is holy to the dogs; nor cast your pearls before swine, lest they trample them under their feet, and turn and tear you in pieces.*" Just so we are clear, this does not mean we should mistreat, abuse, degrade, or shun others; we must always lead in kindness, setting a guard over our tongues and keep it moving in the Spirit of Excellence.

As a Word to the Wise, if we are not exhibiting the Fruits of the Spirit to start, our *Sacredness* is already compromised. Our Spiritual Fruits, Christlike Character, and Our Oneness with the Holy Trinity are our Spiritual Pearls. With all due respect, if we are not leading in such a manner, we have to decide what we are really protecting from the dogs or swine! Here is what 1 Corinthians 3:16-19 says about this matter: "*Do you not know that you are the temple of God and that the Spirit of God dwells in you? If anyone defiles the temple of God, God will destroy him. For the temple of God is holy, which temple you are. Let no one deceive himself. If anyone among you seems to be wise in this age, let him become a fool that he may become wise. For the wisdom of this world is foolishness with God. For it is written, He catches the wise in their own craftiness.*"

Why do we need to become a fool to become wise? Having an open mind for Godly Principles and Protocols does not mean behaving foolishly. Listen, Divine Wisdom is derived from

Spiritual means, and if we want to glean from this type of Wisdom, we must become humble without exhibiting the know-it-all mentality. If we do, we will get second-hand recycled knowledge portrayed as wisdom. In all actuality, it is humanly transferred and not Spirit Transferred.

How do we know the difference between humanly transferred and Spirit Transferred? Divine Wisdom comes with Spiritual Insight, hidden nuggets of Divine Wisdom, Spiritual Instincts, Spiritual Correction, Spiritual Discernment, and the ability to receive Secrets from the Great Unknown. On the other hand, knowledge being portrayed as wisdom is not consistent; it is wavering, unreliable, and pretentious. Why is this the case when faking it? Anyone can relay information they have learned from a book or another person, but it will be full of unsurety.

As a part of our human nature to become the Chosen Ones, we have many people debating or getting angry over the Word of God, especially when no one is 100% right or 100% wrong about our Creator. Is this Biblical? I would have it no other way. *"For My thoughts are not your thoughts, nor are your ways My ways, says the Lord. For as the Heavens are higher than the earth, so are My ways."* Isaiah 55:8-9. The moment we think we have God pegged or above Him, He will change the Spiritual Language to confuse us. If we desire to be *In-The-Spiritual-Know*, we must exhibit humility, cutting through the natural tendencies of our fleshly wants, needs, and desires. Doing so helps to ensure we can Spiritually See, Hear, and Speak correctly without missing our cue or circumventing our Spiritual Anointing.

Now, just so we are clear, we all need knowledge, and knowledge is good to have, but it can change as we evolve. Yet, with the Spirit's intricacies when it comes down to Divine Wisdom, He is absolute and on point, bearing no need to fuss, fight, or debate about Divine Truth, Illumination, or Insight. Besides, this sort of Divine Revelation is for our personal use to guide, protect, and instruct in the commission of our Gifting, Calling, Talent, Purpose, or when bearing the Good News. As a forewarning, it is not for recreational use. Why not? It can become abused, similar to the abuse of power in the worldly realm. Spiritual Abuse is a big no-no in the Kingdom. Using it for worldly corruption will cause us to temporarily or permanently lose Spiritual Access to Divine Wisdom.

According to the *Spiritual Calculations* from the Heavenly of Heavens, it takes a certain type of individual to develop a Direct Connection. What makes this person so unique? They are carrying and being trusted with VITAL INFORMATION from the Kingdom, which cannot be handled in any way, nor can they behave in any way. The person who carries this type of Spiritual Mantle is held at a higher rate of accountability than those still in the Spiritual Classroom learning the Ways of God. Therefore, one should never covet another man's Divine Mission. Why is it not wise to covet? We will never know the weight of the Spiritual Calling or the sacrifice. So, it is best to stay in our lane, doing what we are Divinely Ordained to do without wishing we were someone else.

In developing the *Sacred Art* in the Kingdom, we must begin with a few relational aspects, but not limited to such:

☐ We must effectively relate to God, ourselves, and others to build loyalty and reverence.

☐ We must become excellent listeners to spoken and unspoken words by paying attention, even if we do not feel like it.

☐ We must control our emotions, actions, reactions, and demeanor while responding positively, even if we are offended by something or someone. Doing so helps us master the elements of self-control.

☐ We must stick to the facts at hand without jumping to conclusions. If in doubt, ask fact-finding questions before making assumptions.

- [ ] We must be willing to forgive at the drop of a dime, squashing irrelevant issues while keeping the negative, critical thoughts or inner dialogue at bay.

- [ ] We must be willing to allow people to express themselves without cutting them off, developing a deaf ear, or having the last word.

- [ ] We must become empathetically compassionate with ourselves and others.

- [ ] We must take a moment to think before we speak, react, or debate any issue.

- [ ] We must communicate with clarity to avoid speculation.

- [ ] We must avoid being selfish, fearful, condescending, or creating stumbling blocks.

- [ ] We must be willing to confront and solve problems while avoiding pointing the finger or playing the blame game.

- [ ] We must stay in our own lane while exhibiting the utmost respect for God, ourselves, and others.

When we approach our *Sacredness* from our strengths as opposed to our weaknesses, we are better able to bounce back when or if we fall short or make a mistake. Listen, we are God's *Sacred Creation*, and He has our best interest at heart. Really? Yes, really! For this reason, He allowed Jesus to become a Living Sacrifice for our sake.

The *Sacredness* of the Kingdom relies on the Sovereignty of God to ensure we have what we need in the Realm of the Spirit. What does this mean? The Holy Trinity incorporates the Father, our Creator, the Blood of Jesus as the sacrificial Lamb of God, and the

Holy Spirit as our Divine Guide to help us on this journey called life.

The Kingdom of God is the reason Jesus taught so effectively about our character, how to treat each other, and the reason why we should walk in Faith, Spirit, and Truth, perfecting the *Sacred Art* of grace, sharing, and compassion without abusing the system. In addition, He bridges the gap and breaks the boundaries in Religion by replacing it with the relational factors of Spirituality. Why are relational factors important in the Eye of God? It helps prevent us from going through the motions or division of Religiosity, while not being able to slay our own biases or conquer our kryptonic giants from the inside out. Also, it safeguards us from rejecting those we are called to set an example for or become a Spiritual Ambassador to.

Unbeknown to most, if we overlook what Religion is doing to our human psyche or the box it places us in, it will cause us to secretly, openly, or outright fight against God, ourselves, and others. At the same time, when in denial, secretly struggling from within, or fighting a war of inner trauma, we unawaringly thwart our *Sacredness*, limiting our Spiritual Creativity by default, even if we have the heart to do the right thing. Plus, it contributes to creating all types of blockages, Mentally, Physically, Emotionally, and Spiritually, which adversely affect our people skills without us realizing it, or until it is too late and the damage is already done.

However, all is not lost; Jesus provided hope for us; we have the Holy Spirit to bring light to our areas of darkness, but there is a catch. What is the catch? We must make a conscious choice to AWAKEN our Spirit to become One with the Holy Spirit, exchanging our agenda for a Kingdom one. While simultaneously becoming a work-in-progress by stepping into the Spiritual Classroom to undo the known or unknown conditioning of worldliness.

Now, before we move on, let us take it to scripture, *"Therefore if there is any consolation in Christ, if any comfort of love, if any fellowship of the Spirit, if any affection and mercy, fulfill my joy by being like-minded, having the same love, being of one accord, of one mind. Let nothing be done through selfish* ambition or conceit, but in lowliness of mind let each esteem others better than himself. Let each of you look out not only for his own interests, but also for the interests of others. Let this mind be in you which was also in Christ Jesus." Philippians 2:1-5.

As a part of our *Sacred Art*, we must continue to work on ourselves, *As It Pleases God*. Why should we work on ourselves as Believers? Are we not prepackaged with what we need? When it comes down to the Kingdom of Heaven and our Heaven on Earth Experiences, change is inevitable, and there is always something to learn to promote our Spiritual Growth and Levels. Nonetheless, we are prepackaged with Spiritual Tools and Divine Provisions regarding our Predestined Blueprint, but it does not negate the fact that we must Spiritually Till our own ground. Simply put, we must take action or put in the work to unpack whatever is inside. For example, if we receive a package in the mail, it cannot unpackage itself; we must open the package to benefit from what is inside of it.

Amid all, any growth or level in the Eye of God requires us to become obedient, humble, patient, and peaceful. If not, we will miss vital lessons, information, or understanding. Really? Yes, really! According to the *Spiritual Calculations* of scripture, it says, *"Therefore, my beloved, as you have always obeyed, not as in my presence only, but now much more in my absence, work out your own salvation with fear and trembling; for it is God who works in you both to will and to do for His good pleasure. Do all things without complaining and disputing, that you may become blameless and harmless, children of God without fault in the midst of a crooked and perverse generation, among whom you shine as lights in the world, holding fast the word of life, so that I may rejoice in the day of Christ that I have not run in vain or labored in vain."* Philippians 2:12-16.

For most, they would often think *Sacredness* is unattainable, but I beg to differ. God weighs the contents of our hearts. For example, I am not perfect, yet He uses my Earthen Vessel to reach those who have a sincere desire to become a *Sacred Ambassador* for the Heavenly of Heavens. Why am I chosen for such a task? I work on myself daily to perfect the *Sacred Art* of exhibiting the Fruits of the Spirit,

Christlike Character, humility, and being true to myself while sharing the Good News with clean hands and a pure heart.

By far, if we are willing to step into the Spiritual Classroom with no shame attached, the Holy Spirit will become the Divine Light guiding our every footstep. This Spiritual Principle is similar to the *'cloud by day and the pillar of fire by night'* provided to the Children of Israel without fail while in their *Desert Experience* in Exodus 13:21-22. If we simply embrace this concept, becoming proactive in the Will of God, He will do likewise with us. How do I know? The Sacred Art of this book is all Him, just for you.

Chapter 4

Desert Experience

As a part of life, we will all become enslaved by something or someone, regardless of whether we admit it or not. Although the growth process can become challenging, we must develop our Spiritual Muscles. If not, we become easy prey for the wiles of the enemy or seemingly wounded beyond humanitarian repair. Unbeknown to most, once we become wounded bad enough in our *Desert Experience*, God must intervene on our behalf, circumventing the enemy's plan of having his way with us by giving us the strength needed to move on. The key is to recognize and accept the help when it comes.

The *Desert Experience*, according to the *Spiritual Calculations* of the Heavenly of Heavens, was considered a Spiritual Classroom or Training Ground for the Children of Israel, giving them a bird's eye view of Spiritual Covering through the *'Cloud by Day'* and Divine Illumination through the *'Pillar of Fire by Night.'* Exodus 13:21-22 says, *"And the LORD went before them by day in a pillar of cloud to lead the way, and by night in a pillar of fire to give them light, so as to go by day and night. He did not take away the pillar of cloud by day or the pillar of fire by night from before the people."* Regardless of what we are going through, the provision is already available; however, we must master our ability to effectively tap into it without creating enemies or creating unjustifiable offenses along the way.

Furthermore, if we feel as if we have become wounded beyond repair, we may secretly blame or reject God. Often enough, for whatever reason, this is usually found in those who consider themselves atheists but are not limited to such. Spiritually, they make the best Spiritual Converts. Why is this the case? They know what it is like to be hurt, rejected, abused, ostracized, traumatized, or misused. But the truth of the matter is, they are the ones who become more merciful, caring, forgiving, understanding, and shareable as opposed to being judgmental, irrevocably brow-bashing, or dead-set on rejecting those who are in an inner struggle as they once were.

The truth of the matter is that we will all have a *Desert Experience* at some point, but it does not mean we must wander around clueless or rebellious. If we dare to take heed to the lessons the Children of Israel did or did not learn on their journey into the Promised Land, we can flip the script on our lives in 40 days, as opposed to 40 years. How is it possible to learn from them? Based on their experiences, let me counteract this question with a few others applicable to our lives in today's time:

☐ If God is faithfully providing for us through some means, why would we bite the hand that feeds us?

☐ Why would we symbolically spit in the face of God when He calls us out on our bad behavior?

☐ What would cause our countenance to fall when we do not get what we want?

☐ How can we fix our mouths to complain when God's blessings are evident in our lives?

☐ What would make us contemplate cursing or creating booby-traps for those God has blessed?

☐ Why are we not repenting or apologizing for our wrongdoings, having a bad attitude, or exhibiting appalling character?

- ☐ Is it okay to manipulate, scheme, or bully our way to the top, squashing those who appear beneath us or killing their dreams along the way?

- ☐ What makes us so high-minded to the point we think people should serve us and we do not serve them?

- ☐ How could one think they have the right to violate the free will of another?

- ☐ Is it Christlike to bend the Word of God to condemn, manipulate, or chastise others when we have not taken the time to evaluate our own fruits?

- ☐ Do we think it is okay with God to exhibit covetousness, jealousy, envy, hate, waywardness, or all manner of evil at our leisure?

- ☐ Is it okay to drag our brother or sister through the mud without attempting to pull them out? Or do we think it is wise to kick a person when they are down when it is within our power to help them up or offer them a word of encouragement?

All of these questions are designed to provoke the elements of thought. In my opinion, these are legitimate questions we must answer, especially if we have a Promise attached to our Bloodline. Furthermore, if we have not taken the time to have a little Q and A Session with God, but find all the time in the world to have a Q and A Session with those who may or may not have our best interests at heart, we have work to do.

Not asking the right questions or receiving the right answers will cause inner conflict. How is this possible? If we are not getting an understanding from God's Perspective, we could find ourselves at a loss, piecing our lives together by receiving friendly advice instead of Spiritual Direction.

Of course, we all want what we want, right? We have free will to do so; however, if we are wandering in the desert repeatedly, it is time to get some form of Divine Direction, *As It Pleases God*. If not, it can cause our Promise to overlook us as we wander and wallow in our *Desert Experiences*. Then we may pass it on to the next generation, who are not slaves to negativity, disobedience, pride, or worldliness. What do we need to do? Romans 12:2-3 says it best: *"And do not be conformed to this world, but be transformed by the renewing of your mind, that you may prove what is that good and acceptable and perfect will of God. For I say, through the grace given to me, to everyone who is among you, not to think of himself more highly than he ought to think, but to think soberly, as God has dealt to each one a measure of faith."*

In the commission of the renewing process of our thoughts, behaviors, demeanor, responses, or whatever, it is always best to align it with the Bible or positive affirmations to secure the Promises of God to avoid any form of self-centeredness.

What is the Promise? According to the *Spiritual Calculations* of the Heavenly of Heavens, everyone is different, with various Gifts, Talents, Callings, and Purposes, as well as Spiritual Covenants. Yet, the Covenantal Promise we are dealing with here is: *"And the LORD said, Shall I hide from Abraham what I am doing, since Abraham shall surely become a great and mighty nation, and __All The Nations__ of the earth shall be blessed in him? For I have known him, in order that he may command his children and his household after him, that they keep the way of the LORD, to do righteousness and justice, that the LORD may bring to Abraham what He has spoken to him."* Genesis 18:17-19. What does this mean? We are already Blessed to be a Blessing, but we must hold up our side of the Spiritual Covenant while avoiding any form of hidden or biased agendas.

How does a Spiritual Covenant apply to us in today's day and age? For the simple fact that it states *All The Nations*; it includes us. If we exempt ourselves from our Birthright, we have free will to do so. If our behavior, character, or whatever exempts us, then we cannot blame anyone, right? Absolutely!

So, what is the big hoopla regarding obedience and good behavior? For this question, let me take it to scripture: *"But you are a chosen generation, a royal priesthood, a holy nation, His own special people, that you may proclaim the praises of Him who called you out of darkness into His marvelous light; who once were not a people but are now the people of God, who had not obtained mercy but now have obtained mercy. Beloved, I beg you as sojourners and pilgrims, abstain from fleshly lusts which war against the soul, having your conduct honorable among the Gentiles, that when they speak against you as evildoers, they may, by your good works which they observe, glorify God in the day of visitation. Therefore submit yourselves to every ordinance of man for the Lord's sake, whether to the king as supreme, or to governors, as to those who are sent by him for the punishment of evildoers and for the praise of those who do good. For this is the will of God, that by doing good you may put to silence the ignorance of foolish men—as free, yet not using liberty as a cloak for vice, but as bondservants of God."* 1 Peter 2:9-16.

Our *Desert Experience* is not about a lot of dos and don'ts. It is about surrendering to the Mission of God, getting our flesh out of the way while replacing it with being '*In Purpose On Purpose*,' utilizing the Fruits of the Spirit, and stepping into the Spiritual Classroom to develop Christlike Character. Why do we need to go through all of this? Usually, our *Desert Experience* is of our own making or how we perceive it. The Bible states, *"There is a way that seems right to a man, but its end is the way of death."* Proverbs 14:12.

Spiritually, it is always best to approach people, places, and things from a Godly Perspective. Why should we use a Divine Perspective? We do not know what is lurking around the corner to ensnare us; therefore, it is wise to place God at the forefront of our journey, leading the way, *As It Pleases Him*.

Listen, God is not trying to take our identity or deprive us. Instead, first and foremost, He is helping us establish, unveil, restore, or recognize our worthiness. Secondly, He helps us understand the Divine Order's value by working as a team through the Holy Trinity first, then spreading outwardly. Thirdly, He teaches us how to behave to avoid bringing shame to our names or the Kingdom. With this simple, yet profound *Spiritual Calculation*, when we take possession of our Promise, we will not have to doubt ourselves or God, nor whether He has our best interest at heart.

Now, on the other hand, if we become haughty and resist God in our *Desert Experience*, we can expect a constant bout with a few things:

- ☐ Unfruitfulness.
- ☐ Difficulty.
- ☐ Confusion.
- ☐ Betrayal.
- ☐ Animosity.
- ☐ Anger.
- ☐ Lack of Control.
- ☐ Backlash.
- ☐ Debauchery.
- ☐ Déjà Vu.
- ☐ Hatred.
- ☐ Unforgiveness.

In our *Desert Experiences* or when we are in the Will of God, we may feel all types of negative emotions; still, it is our responsibility to recognize, counteract, or fight them off. Negativity is designed to distract us, making us sick, tired, and weak, zapping our hope. Here is what Proverbs 13:12 says, "*Hope deferred makes the heart sick, but when the desires comes, it is a tree of life.*" The secret behind the lies and deceit of negativity is that God will always turn it around for our good if we do not give in or give up on ourselves, similar to the life of Joseph in the Book of Genesis.

Just remember, God's way up the ladder is not man's way to the top. Once we are established in the Kingdom, and we are '*In Purpose on purpose*,' no man can bring us down unless it is allowed by God Almighty for our benefit. When we are under the Covering of Purpose, God must protect us in our righteousness because "*There is one body and one Spirit, just as you were called in one hope of your calling." Ephesians 4:4.

When operating in Oneness with the Kingdom of Heaven, God will protect what belongs to Him, period. If we do not know this, we can become tricked, deceived, and lured, or someone can easily throw a monkey wrench in our self-esteem to get into our heads. For this reason, we must set a guard over our Mind, Body, Soul, and Spirit, use the Fruits of the Spirit, and exhibit Christlike Character at all times to prevent leaving an open door to become negatively sifted.

Now, on the other hand, if man establishes us, we can become dethroned at any given moment at their pleasure. The obliviousness to this fact will cause us to feed into the negative hoopla or unrestrained lust as opposed to what is positive, productive, and fruitful. What is the cause of this? According to scripture, *"For the flesh lusts against the Spirit, and the Spirit against the flesh; and these are contrary to one another, so that you do not do the things that you wish. But if you are led by the Spirit, you are not under the law."* Galatians 5:17-18.

What do we need to do to keep our rights in the Kingdom of Heaven? We need to pay attention to certain behaviors and avoid getting caught up. Galatians 5:19-21 reminds us of the decree: *"Now the works of the flesh are evident, which are: adultery, fornication, uncleanness, lewdness, idolatry, sorcery, hatred, contentions, jealousies, outbursts of wrath, selfish ambitions, dissensions, heresies, envy, murders, drunkenness, revelries, and the like; of which I tell you beforehand, just as I also told you in time past, that those who practice such things will not inherit the Kingdom of God."*

Why can we not inherit the Kingdom? We need the Spirit to enter and remain in the Kingdom; if we are given away to our lusts without repentance, our Spirit will lie dormant until we come to ourselves, which creates a *Desert Experience* for us, with or without our permission.

Spiritually, in or out of our *Desert Experience*, we must look for the win-win or the positive in all things. Why must we look for the good or the lesson in all things? We never know what God is up to or what is on His Divine Mind. For this reason, keep Jeremiah 29:11 close to the heart at all times: *"For I know the plans I have for you, declares the Lord, plans to prosper you and not to harm you, plans to give you hope and a future."*

It is imperative to work on ourselves from God's Perspective when faced with challenges, especially when the hot, scorching *Desert Experience* is staring us right in the face. Listed below are a few clues we can glean regarding His Spiritual method of operation with the Children of Israel, but not limited to such:

- ☐ He will hide us in an *'Egypt,'* causing us to cry out repentantly or to see if we will settle where we do not belong.

- ☐ He will provide a *'Red Sea Experience'* to see if we will move forward in confidence or retreat out of the lack of faith.

- ☐ He will provide a *'Cloud by Day'* to cover us to see if we will recognize or ignore it.

- ☐ He will provide *'Fire by Night'* to guide us to see if we will follow or rebel.

- ☐ He will provide *'Manna'* as a provision to see if we are grateful or ungrateful.

- ☐ He will provide a *'Moses'* to instruct us to see if we will obey or become self-serving.

- ☐ He will provide an *'Aaron'* to fill in the gap of weakness to see if we will accept or reject help.

- ☐ He will provide a *'Jethro'* to advise, mentor, or coach us to see if we will take heed to someone wiser in a different area or develop a deaf ear.

- [ ] He will provide '*Quails*' to test our level of lustful greed, to see if we will exercise self-control or over-indulge instead.

- [ ] He will provide '*Water in the rock*' to see if we will follow instructions or become angrily impatient while on Spiritual Assignment.

- [ ] He will provide '*Spies*' to go before us to spy out the land to see if we will settle for defeat or come back with a '*Joshua and Caleb*' report of victory, Mentally, Physically, Emotionally, and Spiritually.

- [ ] He will provide a '*Wall of Jericho*' to test our faithful obedience, to see if we will sync ourselves with Divine Timing or worldly timing.

Whether we are in our *Egypt*, wandering in our *Desert*, or in our *Promised Land*, God likes us to dig deep into the Spiritual Realm. Why are we harping on this Spiritual Stuff? We are Spirit first, having a human experience. To transform back into how we were created in the first place, God hides our '*Treasures*' to test us, ensuring we understand who we are and not settle for things at face value or become trapped in mediocrity.

Our Heaven on Earth Experience keeps our mental wheels turning in the right direction to avoid complacency, ungratefulness, idolatry, and worldliness. So, when the '*Amalekites*' come to war against us while we are in our *Desert Experience*, we will have the strategic ability to put on the Whole Armor of God with uplifted hands to fight for what rightly belongs to us.

Why do we have to fight as Believers? It is not a physical fight; we will go into Spiritual Warfare to protect our Divine Dominion, while fighting with the Holy Trinity, the Word of God, the Fruits of the Spirit, and Christlike Character. These Spiritual Tools and

Weapons work and are foolproof if we learn how to use them, *As It Pleases God*.

In the Spiritual Realm, Blessings of Capacity are not handed to us on a silver platter. We would not understand the value or the sacrifice; therefore, ungratefulness can easily cause us to become irresponsible, critical, negative, judgmental, and unmerciful.

Spiritually, if we keep ourselves on the positive side of the spectrum along with a Positive Mental Attitude, we will never have to doubt the Promises of God. How can we possibly not have doubt? We will all have our moments of doubt or uncertainty. The 'what-ifs' and the fear of the unknown are built into our DNA to save our lives with an alarm system, not to take our lives with Spiritual Paralysis. As this is an inevitable part of life, we must know and understand the difference to overcome, *As It Pleases God*. Without the fragments of doubt, it is impossible to build genuine faith. So let us focus on walking by faith, and not by sight, exhibiting gratefulness in all things, including the Breath of Life. It has a way of shutting the mouth of doubtfulness.

We are living and walking in the Promises without realizing it or genuinely taking possession of them. What do we need to do to unveil our realization? Begin using the Fruits of the Spirit faithfully from Galatians 5:22-26: *"But the fruit of the Spirit is love, joy, peace, longsuffering, kindness, goodness, faithfulness, gentleness, self-control. Against such there is no law. And those who are Christ's have crucified the flesh with its passions and desires. If we live in the Spirit, let us also walk in the Spirit. Let us not become conceited, provoking one another, envying one another."*

By focusing on staying positive, productive, and fruitful, we will begin to understand what is required of us from a Kingdom Perspective by default. What does this mean? Most of us focus solely on not being negative or a bad person; therefore, it takes all of our energy. As a result, we forget about simply being positive, which, in my opinion, is not wise.

Listen, if we place more of our energy on the positive, then more of our fruits will become positive, giving us more power to counteract the negative. For example, the Fruits of the Spirit (Love, Joy, Peace, Patience, Kindness, Goodness, Faithfulness, Gentleness, and Self-Control) are all positive qualities. If we use them and repent when we use them amiss, we will naturally become better people by Divine Default. How is this humanly possible? They are already wired into our DNA; they are buried under layers of debris, trauma, conditioning, or biases.

Not using the Fruits of the Spirit does not necessarily make us a bad person; however, it does cause us to become misunderstood, misrepresented, misused, mistreated, or outright miss the mark, especially in our *Desert Experience*. Now, according to the *Spiritual Calculations* of the Heavenly of Heavens, to experience the Fullness of the Kingdom, listed below are a few items to work on, but not limited to such:

- ☐ We must become Spirit-Led, Christlike, and forgiving.
- ☐ We must become proactive, loyal, and diligent.
- ☐ We must become wise, courageous, and humbly confident.
- ☐ We must become decisive, assertive, and consistent.
- ☐ We must become timely, organized, and strategic.
- ☐ We must become creative, open-minded, and knowledgeable.
- ☐ We must become flexible, disciplined, and skilled.
- ☐ We must become truthful, compassionate, and full of integrity.
- ☐ We must become instinctual, negotiating, and fluent.
- ☐ We must become motivational, encouraging, and inspirational.
- ☐ We must become a planner, communicator, and teacher.
- ☐ We must become comfortable in the skin we are in while using our Gifts, Calling, or Talents with no regrets.

We do not have to become all of these at one time; one step at a time will do the trick. Better yet, if we take one step a week, in 12 weeks, one would be amazed at the debris that unearths our Spiritual Fruits.

If we fall short, it is our responsibility to ask or seek help. Why do we need help as Believers? God tests us through people; therefore, if we fall short in our People Skills, we may fall short in our Spiritual Cooperative Skills. All this means is that our teachability, correctability, and awareness will be generated from our communicative or relational people problems. The last thing we would ever want to do in or out of our *Desert Experience* is to develop *Spiritual Amnesia* as the Children of Israel did. What does *Spiritual Amnesia* have to do with anything? It blocks our Blessings, causing the enemy to have a field day with our tattered thoughts, ungoverned emotions, and unfulfilled desires.

Listen, Moses was not an alien or some super-being; he was a mere mortal like you and me. What God did for and through Moses is available to those who are willing to put in the work to achieve, using the Spiritual Tools in hand. Now, if you are ready, let us go deeper.

Chapter 5

Spiritual Amnesia

As we are here in today's time, according to the *Spiritual Calculations* of the Ancient, our point of *Spiritual Origin* begins in the Book of Genesis. Unbeknown to most, the hardwire of our DNA is grafted into the web of the Garden of Eden, linking us to where we are right now. The Ancients of Ancients want us to take the time to remember what we may have forgotten through the ages. And if we dare to embrace the Divine Wisdom already hidden within, we will find the Spiritual Principles needed for such a time as this. But more importantly, making this long-awaited Spiritual Connection gives us the ability to open the Spiritual Seals in the Book of Revelation with the Kingdom Credentials needed from the Heavenly of Heavens.

Unbeknown to most, the Divine Instructions from the Heavenly of Heavens are already written on the Tablet of our Hearts, even if we have developed some form of amnesia. What does this mean? We already know this information; we have developed worldly amnesia, preventing us from coming to ourselves or remembering who we are and why. Or, we may suffer from Spiritual Amnesia, which prevents us from fully connecting to the Source from a Heavenly Perspective due to some form of Religiosity, bias, title, unrepentance, or privilege. What does this mean? We have one foot in the Church and one foot out, or we are bound to conditioning or traditions as opposed to having a Spiritual Relationship with God, *As It Pleases Him*.

Spiritual Amnesia can work for or against us, especially if we become oblivious to our inherent Blessings right before our very eyes. However, if we learn to become balanced from the inside out, we can better govern our level of amnesia as the Holy Spirit permits. Although we have two types of amnesia, worldly and Spiritual, we must understand them, *As It Pleases God*.

According to the *Spiritual Calculations* of the Heavenly of Heavens, when it comes down to our Promise, Purpose, Birthrights, Blessings, or Bloodline, we will be dealing with the two factors of Spiritual Amnesia:

- ☐ *Factor One*: We need to develop *Covered Amnesia* to protect our sanity, livelihood, or well-being to move forward with our Promise, *As It Pleases God*. Often, these are found in using the Fruits of the Spirit and exhibiting Christlike Character. In my opinion, they are like Spiritual Buffers, keeping us from wrecking ourselves and the lives of others. In addition, *Covered Amnesia* will also protect us from the malicious attempts of the enemy designed to destroy us Mentally, Physically, Emotionally, or Spiritually, causing all things to work together for our good.

- ☐ *Factor Two*: There is also *Traumatizing Amnesia* we develop to protect ourselves from further trauma, or it is also our internal instinctual red flag. How do we make this make sense, especially as Believers? We have an internal sensor designed to naturally kick in to protect us by any means necessary. Spiritually, if we do not learn how to make this factor of amnesia work on our behalf, it could become our detriment. We could easily harbor negative emotions without realizing it. At the same time, developing negative character traits as a form of protection by inadvertently building walls, as opposed to instituting positive ones to break barriers.

With *Traumatizing Amnesia*, we need to regraft its core by cultivating the power hidden in our ability to forgive, repent, extend mercy, share love, and offer compassion wholeheartedly. Doing so will prevent any form of yokes, bondages, soul ties, or enslavement, Mentally, Physically, Emotionally, or Spiritually, preventing us from our Promise or causing us to become oblivious to it.

Spiritual Amnesia has been around for centuries, doing what it is designed to do. What was it designed to do? Contrary to what most would think, when it comes down to amnesia, it is designed to bring awareness. How is this possible when amnesia causes us to forget? When dealing with Spiritual Means from the Heavenly of Heavens and *As It Pleases God*, we play by different rules.

Although forgetting plays a factor in Spiritual Amnesia, it promotes the desire to remember as well. We *'forget to remember'* and *'we remember to forget'* as a part of our uniqueness; however, if the Holy Spirit is not involved, our approach to this process can become very tricky, ensnaring those who do not understand the intricacies associated with our perceptions, *As It Pleases God*.

For example, when the Holy Spirit is involved, we forget the negative through forgiving and repentance to remember the Promises of God. And we remember the Promises of God to forget about the negativity to focus on the positive aspects of life. Now, without the Holy Spirit involved, we forget about what God has done for us to remember all of the pain and negativity. And, we remember how life has tossed us to and fro, forgetting the many Blessings hidden in plain sight. Therefore, when dealing with any form of amnesia, incorporating the Holy Spirit into the equation is always the right thing to do. Why must we use the Holy Spirit as a Spiritual Buffer? When used correctly, the Holy Spirit keeps us from hurting ourselves without realizing what we are doing. Plus, He helps us understand the reasons why we are doing it as well.

The Children of Israel contributed to their inner trauma due to their perception of Moses, while not taking into consideration the *Spiritual Calculations* of God. As a result of this miscalculation, as well as the cancerous cell of idolatry imprinted in their psyche from being in Egypt, the default mechanism hidden in their Spiritual Amnesia kicked in, causing them to stray negatively. As a result, they built a golden calf to worship, satiating an inner longing or thirst to have a right-now god, which caused a Spiritual Setback on their behalf. Why would this happen? Frankly, they were not Mentally, Physically, Emotionally, or Spiritually ready for the Kingdom Commission. Simply put, they were suffering from Spiritual Amnesia, forgetting about the Miracles of God as well as the Spiritual Vessel sent by Him to guide, teach, train, and protect them. More importantly, they forgot about how God prepared Moses for their sake.

In my opinion, as a family man, finessed with Egyptian Principles, if it were up to Moses, he would have remained with his family herding sheep. Frankly, this is why he made all types of excuses at the Burning Bush. What type of excuses did he make?

- ☐ Excuse One: He was slow of speech. Moses lived for 40 years in royalty in Egypt and 40 years in the desert, talking to sheep all day. In my opinion, he was not that slow of speech. Eighty years of living is a long time to communicate. In my opinion, a little stutter does not stop a show, nor will it stop God. The Voice of God is crystal clear, but He will use some form of an impediment, testing our devotion to the Mission. Nevertheless, due to his willingness, God gave him a mouthpiece through his brother Aaron with specific instructions.

- ☐ Excuse Two: The people would not believe God sent him to deliver them. If the Children of Israel were already living on a wing and a prayer, why would they not believe? It was not the people not believing...Moses was in disbelief. However, God provided him with confirmation to satiate his insecurities by telling His people 'I Am' sent him. Then, perform specific revelatory signs using the transformation of his rod and the leprous hand in front of them. Did it make a believer out of them? It did, but in my opinion, it made more of a believer out of Moses.

- Excuse Three: The Egyptians would kill him. In my opinion, this is one of the biggest excuses of them all. If the Egyptians wanted to find Moses, they would have found him, just like they found him and the Children of Israel at the Red Sea before crossing. The question remains: Did they even search for him after killing a Hebrew enslaved person? From my perspective, he was more afraid of his own kind wiping him out. So, the question is, was he running from Pharaoh or the people whom he was called to deliver? Regardless of which side of the fence he was running from, God commissioned him to do a job.

According to the *Spiritual Calculations* from the Heavenly of Heavens, regardless of how they felt about Moses, their wailing cry called him out of his *Spiritual Nesting Phase* into Purpose. So, the question is, 'How could they possibly develop Spiritual Amnesia, especially after all the preparation that came with bringing Moses to the forefront?' What was the preparation process for Moses?

- God saved him from being killed as a child.

- God strategically placed him in the Pharaoh's house to glean wisdom.

- God intuitively gave him two mothers to train him in Egyptian and Hebrew Culture.

- God inducted him into royalty to develop a Kingdom Mentality.

- God purposefully trained him as a warrior for combat from a Mental, Physical, Emotional, and Spiritual Realm.

- ☐ God intentionally allowed him to turn on the Egyptian royal family to break the bond and become trained in dealing with a yoked or untrained mentality through herding sheep.

- ☐ God cleverly ushered him into the wilderness to retrain him in Kingdom Principles by leading sheep.

- ☐ God ingeniously allowed him to reflect on how to protect and serve the Kingdom through herding sheep before shepherding God's sheep.

- ☐ God distinctly created an opportunity for him to learn that His presence is a *Sacred Space* and that respect must be initiated.

- ☐ God resourcefully placed him alone to hear himself speak while correcting his inner chatter and doubt as he transitioned into his Divine Mission at the Burning Bush.

- ☐ God tenaciously gave him the ability to restructure, strategize, facilitate, dictate, and conquer by putting on the Whole Armor of God to win the freedom of the Children of Israel.

- ☐ God allowed his blemishes to facilitate an intimate relationship with Him, learning the value of repenting, fasting, prayer, and intercession from the Heavenly of Heavens to create miracle upon miracle.

Although these are not directly stated in scripture, they are stated in a factual psychological nature. What does this mean? The *Spiritual Calculations* of God are Absolute, and in order to get to a certain Level of Spirituality or be allowed to accomplish specific tasks in the Kingdom, one must go through a Spiritual Classroom. If one fails, the lesson is repeated until our formulation comes up with the right calculation before commencement can take place. Yet, after all is said and done, one would agree that the Spiritual Calculations of Moses' life were DIVINELY STRATEGIC. In my opinion, no one besides God Almighty could have planned it any better.

If we take a moment to think, although Moses was not perfect, he was effectively obedient, knowing beyond a shadow of a doubt that God's Divine Mission would be fulfilled through him. With this knowledge, he did not know how, when, or where, but he knew two things about God:

- ☐ He knew WHAT God was going to do. He was going to deliver His people out of bondage.

- ☐ He knew WHY God was going to do it. The Children of Israel were God's Chosen People, and He was going to make good on His PROMISE.

The Signs and Wonders of God are all around us, regardless of whether we are conditioned to see them or not. But let me say this before moving on: When looking from the outside in, and if our mind is enslaved, we will not appreciate the Leading of the Lord, period. However, if we begin to take a look at ourselves and our lives from the inside out, we are better able to see what God has done and continues to do.

More importantly, regardless of whether we bring science into the equation of Spirituality, the Word of God is given as a Spiritual Compass to guide, teach, correct, and inspire us through the leading of the Holy Spirit. If we digress in this formality or refuse the Spiritual Classroom, we will not receive all God has for us.

There are HIDDEN LESSONS in the Word of God that we must learn, understand, or obey. If we overlook the *Spiritual Calculations* it possesses, Spiritual Amnesia will become prominent, even if we attempt to cover it up or we feel right in our own eyes. How is this possible? It is filtered through the lusts of the flesh, the lust of the eyes, and the pride of life, which causes Spiritual Blindness, Deafness, and Muteness.

How can we make Spiritual Amnesia work on our behalf? We can make it work on our behalf if we pay attention to the moral Code of Conduct for the Kingdom of Heaven, use the Fruits of the Spirit, and invoke the Holy Trinity (The Father, Son, and Holy Spirit) in our lives. In addition, He will send us a sign through a seemingly *Burning Bush Experience*, making His presence known. This usually happens when we are alone in His presence while meditating on the Word of God. Why are we most often alone? It helps us to avoid distractions that drown out the gentle whispers of God, to avoid the riffraff (the undesirable people who are not privy to the Plan of God in our lives), or to cancel the negative and monitoring influences that we do not fully understand as of yet.

The Word of God helps us align our Spiritual Experiences, and if we are clueless, we may miss the mark or misinterpret the people, places, and things of God or what is not of Him.

What would cause us to miss the mark or misinterpret, especially when our heart posture is upright? The reasons will vary on a sliding scale depending on our Spiritual Instincts or Understanding. Rest assured, if we are not appropriately synced with the Elements of God, *As It Pleases Him*, our Spiritual Compass will not calibrate properly.

As it relates to *Spiritual Calculations*, God will always give us a *Spiritual Rod* or place something in our hands, as He did with Moses, to use in the commission of His Divine Mission. Why are we given something to work with? If He calls us to complete a particular task, He will equip, correct, and train us in the ways and repercussions of its use. On the other hand, if we DO NOT recognize the Divine Mission or we take our Spiritual Tools for granted, then, unfortunately, we cannot blame another for our Spiritual Negligence or Amnesia.

The bottom line is that when it is all said and done, what is and what will be, is already. Therefore, it is always best to get the *Spiritual Calculations* correct by leaning on the Holy Spirit to unveil the areas we are veiled to fill our Spiritual Baskets, *As It Pleases God*.

Chapter 6

Spiritual Baskets

The *Spiritual Calculations* have been in motion since the BEGINNING of time, letting us know this one fact: God is still on the Throne regardless of our rationality or nationality. We can deceive ourselves into believing whatever or whomever we like, but we have Spiritual Rules and Protocols when it comes down to the Kingdom of Heaven. We do not need someone to differentiate between right and wrong; we already know it! Good and evil are written on the Tablet of our Hearts, giving us a choice between a worldly or *Spiritual Basket* and what we put in or take out of it.

Now, if we decide God's way is not for us, we can revoke our privileges at the drop of a dime without the Spiritual Benefits of the Kingdom being at the forefront of our lives. Yet, at the same time, we must also keep in mind that our *Spiritual Baskets* become worldly if we mix our fruits in the SAME basket.

Basically, if we want all the Kingdom has for us, we must master the ability to keep worldly fruits outside of our *Spiritual Baskets* to ensure the rottenness does not get inside of us. Without biases, rejecting, or hurting others, Romans 12:2 cloaks us with responsibility: *"Do not be conformed to this world, but be transformed by the renewing of your mind, that you may prove what is good and acceptable and perfect will of God."* More importantly, if misbehaving, rejecting others out of unkindness, or pompousness is flowing from our baskets, we must check the source.

Unbeknown to most, the *Spiritual Calculatory* equational factors in life are predicated on something or someone, keeping us grounded in our Earthly Experiences through the use of our people skills. It is God's way of accomplishing a specific Spiritual Mission using our inner-born relational apparatuses. When our relational skills are used correctly or in the way God intended, they prevent us from becoming a basket case of worldliness.

How can I call someone a basket case? First, I am not speaking directly to a person; I am referring to a worldly condition of the human psyche. Secondly, when our minds become trapped in a box with waywardness or debauchery, it is often referred to as having our heads in a basket. Thirdly, God will give us a choice of choosing the case (our environment), which will enclose our baskets as well. Really? Yes, really!

To avoid confusion or misrepresentation, let me Spiritual Align the basket theme from Jeremiah 24:1-3: *"The LORD showed me, and there were two baskets of figs set before the temple of the LORD, after Nebuchadnezzar king of Babylon had carried away captive Jeconiah the son of Jehoiakim, king of Judah, and the princes of Judah with the craftsmen and smiths, from Jerusalem, and had brought them to Babylon. One basket had very good figs, like the figs that are first ripe; and the other basket had very bad figs which could not be eaten, they were so bad. Then the LORD said to me, 'What do you see, Jeremiah?' And I said, Figs, the good figs, very good; and the bad, very bad, which cannot be eaten, they are so bad."*

According to the *Spiritual Calculations* of the Heavenly of Heavens, we have two free-will choices of baskets:

- ☐ We have the opportunity to become a worldly basket case, drawn away by our lusts, thoughts, and emotions. Unfortunately, this allows us to willfully remove God from the equation of our Divine Existence, contributing to all types of known and unknown curses with negative, rotten, and destructive fruits, instigating division or violence. We can read all about it in Zachariah 5:1-11.

☐ We have the opportunity to become a *Spiritual Basket* for the Kingdom, incorporating God into the equation of our Divine Existence, *As It Pleases Him*. Fortunately, this allows us to create known and unknown Blessings full of the Fruits of the Spirit, Christlike Character, and peaceful Oneness.

How can we equate anything relating to God with baskets? Baskets were used before we became accustomed to our new way of doing things, but in today's terms, we refer to baskets as carts. For the *Spiritual Calculations* of our fruits, we will use *Spiritual Baskets* to tie in the Word of God, unveiling its importance in the Kingdom.

How do we add the Kingdom to the *Spiritual Equation* of our baskets? In the Eye of God, our *Spiritual Basket* is not an ordinary basket; it has a Purpose. But do not take my word for it; let us align it with scripture: *"And it shall be, when you come into the land which the LORD your God is giving you as an inheritance, and you possess it and dwell in it, that you shall take some of the first of all the produce of the ground, which you shall bring from your land that the LORD your God is giving you, and put it in a basket and go to the place where the LORD your God chooses to make His name abide."* Deuteronomy 26:1-2.

According to the *Spiritual Calculations* of the Heavenly of Heavens, if we use our *Spiritual Baskets* properly, our Blessings will multiply. To start, we can begin with the Miracle of Jesus feeding a multitude of people. Here is the scripture: *"When it was evening, His disciples came to Him, saying, 'This is a deserted place, and the hour is already late. Send the multitudes away, that they may go into the villages and buy themselves food.' But Jesus said to them, 'They do not need to go away. You give them something to eat.' And they said to Him, 'We have here only five loaves and two fish.' He said, 'Bring them here to Me.' Then He commanded the multitudes to sit down on the grass. And He took the five loaves and the two fish, and looking up to heaven, He blessed and broke and gave the loaves to the disciples; and the disciples gave to the multitudes. So they all ate and were filled, and they took up twelve baskets full of the fragments that remained. Now those who had eaten were about five thousand men, besides women and children."* Matthew 14:15-21.

Some countries still use baskets to carry items on their heads. Why do people carry things on their heads? The head is a lot stronger, strategically calculated, and more balanced than we give it credit for. If we are not accustomed to using our heads in such a manner, this sort of feat would be a challenge. The use of this same concept applies to Spiritual Principles when carrying a *Spiritual Basket* on our heads as well. If one can recall, Joseph interpreted the chief baker's dream regarding three baskets in Genesis 40:16-23.

What made this dream so significant? Joseph knew the value of the head. What does this mean? Without the head, the body dies in the Spiritual Realm and in reality. In the dream, if birds were eating from the basket on the chief baker's head, it is a Divine Sign of death in reality. All manifestations are Spirit first, long before making their way to reality. According to the *Spiritual Calculations*, if the chief baker had repented of his wrongdoings, asking for forgiveness without trying to whitewash it or bringing the innocent chief butler into his lies, it would have changed the trajectory of the outcome. Yet, instead, he chose to die with his lies.

What about the chief butler? Now that the value has been established regarding the power of our heads, let us move to the hand. First and foremost, our fruitfulness will not always remain on or in our heads; it will also be in our hands as well. This Spiritual Precept is similar to Joseph's interpretation of the chief butler's dream of having the Pharaoh's cup restored into his hands in Genesis 40:8-15. More importantly, there was also an agreement when the dream was conveyed to the chief butler. What was it? It was 'Remember me.'

Joseph knew the *Spiritual Calculations* of God and the intricacies lying in the power of agreement; therefore, he created a Spiritual Covenant with the Fruits he possessed in his *Spiritual Basket*. What was it? It was the Gift of Interpretation and Prophecy, providing a platform for him to bring revelatory information to Pharaoh in Genesis 41 when the time was right. If he had gotten recognition at the wrong time, his timing would have been off. According to

His Divine Timing, God will always provide a Spiritual Tool, Gift, Calling, or Talent to bring us to our Purpose.

Regardless of the types of Baskets of Fruit that we are working with, when it comes down to becoming well-calculated, we should always incorporate the *Spiritual Calculations* of the Kingdom, *As It Pleases God*. Exhibiting good, positive charactorial qualities ensures we bring forth blessings instead of known or unknown curses out of negligence. How do we know if this is Biblical before we put in the work? It says, *"He shall be like a tree planted by the rivers of water, that brings forth its fruit in its season, whose leaf also shall not wither; and whatever he does shall prosper. The ungodly are not so, but are like the chaff which the wind drives away."* Psalm 1:3-4. What does a tree have to do with us? Like a tree, we are designed to dig our roots deep, grow, reproduce, and prosper with the Spiritual Water from the Heavenly of Heavens. If we digress in this formality, with time, we will become brittle, blown away by the least amount of wind (stress, trauma, fear, defeat, and rejection).

The moment we exempt the Holy Trinity (The Father, Son, and Holy Spirit) from the equation of our lives, we have to keep everything together on our own while avoiding becoming unglued at the seams from the vicissitudes of life. Does it work? It may work for a while through worldly means, but we will eventually grow weary in due season, laying blame similar to the behaviors of Adam and Eve in the Garden of Eden.

Why do we engage in the blaming game? To the natural eye, it appears easier to blame another for unmet expectations, the perceived notion of failure, or the onset of some form of shame, as opposed to assuming responsibility or repenting. Of course, we are all guilty of pointing the finger at some point because it is in our nature to do so. If we look at children for a moment, they will naturally point the finger in their wrongdoing. If left uncorrected, it will continue into adulthood, hindering their ability to resolve problems effectively or assume responsibility.

When our baskets are empty, we will begin to question our worthiness as we lose hope. We are created to serve others, and if we are wallowing in secret desperation, we exude this in the lives of others by being too clingy, too radical, too emotional, too unhinged, too disrespectful, too controlling, or too whatever. I know the word desperation has a negative connotation, but if we dig deep within our souls, we may find that this one contributing factor is spoiling our fruits.

In essence, when we are secretly on a slippery slope, we know it! Most often, we use habits, materialism, or some form of worldliness as a potential cover-up. Sadly, there are times we do not realize we are doing this to ourselves. Why not? We have been veiled, not seeing what is in plain sight. In the *Spiritual Calculations*, all is not lost—let us go deeper.

Our baskets will contain miracles or miraculous pacifiers. What is the difference? One is Divinely Orchestrated, and the other is self-orchestrated. For example, we can 'Be a Blessing' for the Kingdom of Heaven, or we can force the 'Illusion of a Blessing' to appease others.

Spiritually, if God performed a Supernatural Miracle before our very eyes, we would be in disbelief. For our sake, this is why God will most often perform His Miracles when we are not looking. Why does He hide things from the view of Believers? The fear of the Supernatural can traumatize us, leaving us shaking in our boots if we are not accustomed to all things Spiritual.

To preserve our sanity, we are Spiritually Developed in stages to get us accustomed to the Principalities of Spiritual Consonance (Balanced Harmony in the Realm of the Spirit). If not, we can overturn our *Spiritual Baskets* due to some form of Spiritual Negligence. How does this make sense when we are careful, faithful, and diligent? Through the misuse of our Spiritual Power for selfish means or gain, which is often referred to as 'abusing the system' or 'crying wolf' at our pleasure. For the sake of mankind, we are granted a *Spiritual Basket* to Divinely Cover us, which is hidden within the brain. Really? Yes, really!

Picturesquely, if we can visualize turning our brain upside down, it will also give the appearance of a basket. Why should we envision our brain as a *Spiritual Basket*? It is holding something valuable beyond what we could ever imagine. The hardware for our existence is often overlooked because we are trained to depend upon our earthly system as opposed to the Heavenly of Heavens. What does this mean? Our Earthen Vessel is designed with the *Spiritual Calculations* needed to make us a Genius; yet, due to our lack of understanding, we put our brain in a box, only using ten percent or less of it.

On the other hand, if we are wayward or evil, our Genius Capabilities percentage is less due to Spiritual Blockages. In this state, when we feel secretly or openly deprived, we have to manipulate the system or go to the dark side to appear as if we are more astute than we really are. How can I say such a thing, right? Here is what 2 Peter 1:5-9 says: *"But also for this very reason, giving all diligence, add to your faith virtue, to virtue knowledge, to knowledge self-control, to self-control perseverance, to perseverance godliness, to godliness brotherly kindness, and to brotherly kindness love. For if these things are yours and abound, you will be neither barren nor unfruitful in the knowledge of our Lord Jesus Christ. For he who lacks these things is shortsighted, even to blindness, and has forgotten that he was cleansed from his old sins."*

How can we use more than ten percent of our brains? Listed below are a few ways, but not limited to such:

☐ We must understand who we are and why from a Spiritual Perspective through the Spiritual Awakening Process.

☐ We must come to an understanding that we are Spirit, first.

☐ We must be willing and able to apply the Word of God in our daily lives.

☐ We must read as a form of mental stimulation, removing all negative cobwebs.

☐ We must consistently use the Fruits of the Spirit while exhibiting Christlike Character.

- ☐ We must be willing to become truthful and transparent with God, ourselves, and others.

- ☐ We must be willing to ask fact-finding questions, seek Divine Answers, and find a way to become positively proactive for the Kingdom.

- ☐ We must be willing to do the right thing, even if we are booted out of the majority.

- ☐ We must be willing to become the Spiritual Vessel God uses to bless, help, feed, or nurture His sheep.

- ☐ We must become faithful, diligent, obedient, and confident with our Gifting, Calling, Talent, or Mission, weeding out the dream killers.

- ☐ We must tame the negative chatter from within by replacing it with positive affirmations or uplifting scriptures.

- ☐ We must be willing to become Spiritually Unveiled to ignite our instinctual nature to become ONE with the Holy Spirit for the guidance needed on this journey.

The Fruits of our Baskets are in high demand, even if it is not voiced accordingly. What does this mean? A stranger is not going to walk up to us saying, 'I need a hug today,' 'I am having a challenging day,' 'I really need a word of encouragement,' or 'I need someone to make my day.' However, they will patronize the people, places, and things possessing the natural flow of what they secretly need.

What does this have to do with our brains? When our brains are stimulated with kindness, compassion, and mercy, we respond internally, even if we have a heart of stone or whether we are the giver or receiver. More importantly, when using the Fruits of the

Spirit and Christlike Character, it must flow naturally like a stream of water. If not, it can break the elements of trust.

Our responses are fruits that have the power to make or break someone's day. When our *Spiritual Basket* is filled with the right fruits, causing people to feel good, loved, or wanted, we can change the trajectory of a person's day, even if we do not know them. For example, Chick-fil-A is one of the fastest-growing fast-food chains in the nation.

Although their food is good, this is not the only reason why people flock to this restaurant; they come for the serviceable feeling. What does this mean? The kindness of their employees is an expectation for customers through their slogan of response, 'My Pleasure.' If one does not believe it, check the numbers. If one receives another response other than 'My Pleasure,' they will feel slighted in some way. For this reason, this food chain makes the *Spiritual Calculations* of their vetting process strategic, precise, and charactorial. I am not here to promote one restaurant over another, but **consistent** charactorial positivity goes a long way when doing business. Customers will go out of their way to support what makes their day, even if it is for a few seconds.

As we look around, we see that all types of baskets are adorned quite well; however, if we do not take a moment to analyze the fruits inside the basket, we can become deceived. The fruits can be rotten to the core with jealousy, envy, pride, coveting, bitterness, debauchery, household or public idols, and the list goes on. And if we are not careful, we can buy into the fruit of good and evil, getting us tossed to and fro when our intentions are pure. Is this Biblical? Of course, 1 Peter 5:5-7 says, *"Likewise you younger people, submit yourselves to your elders. Yes, all of you be submissive to one another, and be clothed with humility, for 'God resists the proud, but gives grace to the humble.' Therefore humble yourselves under the mighty hand of God, that He may exalt you in due time, casting all your care upon Him, for He cares for you."*

When operating in a Contrite Spirit, we help our instincts pick up on the silent clues of debauched character. How? Most people think repenting is for the weak, but it is totally the opposite—it is for the strong. The strength of our *Spiritual Basket* is not weft with pride, arrogance, rudeness, or any form of leprous behavior; it is weft with humility, peace, mercy, and forgiveness. According to the *Spiritual Calculations* of the Kingdom, Leviticus 13 explains in detail how our weft baskets or garments are determined either clean or unclean by what is oozing out of us.

Contrary to what we are conditioned to think, negative behavior is like an unseen plague, engulfing those who are oblivious to its method of operation. What does the Book of Leviticus have to do with us in today's day and age? Spiritually, it has everything to do with us, especially when everything is now turned inward toward the human psyche.

Spiritual Blindness, Deafness, and Muteness keep us veiled from seeing, hearing, or understanding the obvious Spiritual Cues given to assist us through our instinctual nature, *As It Pleases God*. So, we must examine ourselves accordingly to ensure we do not become a victim and we are not injecting harmful toxins into the lives of those who are not aware of their weaknesses or biases.

Chapter 7

Spiritual Calculations

Forgetting God is not an option for those who desire to glean from the Heavenly of Heavens. If one has not noticed by now, the *Spiritual Calculations* of Genesis 1 are not equated to anything we can do in our own strength. God was very specific in what He desired from His *Earthly Project*, preventing us from playing god in the future. Then, in the *Spiritual Calculations* of Genesis 2, He gives us specific details of His *Personal Project*, Adam and Eve, as well as the Spiritual Protocols and Instructions needed for them to remain and be fruitful. Although this information's relevance may be antiquated for some, it is relevant for the Kingdom, regardless of our perception.

In the *Spiritual Calculations*, the Garden of Eden is hidden within us. If we violate our own Garden, we will find ourselves running from the enemy from within while attempting to make everyone around us do likewise.

The moment we begin to apply the *Spiritual Calculations* from the Heavenly of Heavens to our lives, we change for the better automatically, regardless of our weaknesses, traumas, faults, or biases. Although it may not be an overnight process, it is indeed well worth the effort. It helps to revamp our lives Mentally, Physically, Emotionally, and Spiritually, even if we feel as if we have it all together.

The *Spiritual Calculations* of God do not require us to hit people over the head with the Bible; they require us to lead by example with the Fruits of the Spirit in hand while exhibiting Christlike Character. What does this mean? If we work on ourselves first, our Spiritual Light will begin to illuminate the lives of others by default; however, we must know and understand what will cause our dimness as well.

The mathematical equations of the Spirit are nothing to play around with. The Spirit of God is Absolute; even if we interject mercy or grace into the equation, it does not remove consequences; however, it may lessen them if we master the *Spiritual Calculatory Process*. What does this mean? Repentance is necessary. If we use the Fruits of the Spirit in conjunction with Christlike Character, pursuing the Will of God, it does not remove accountability; however, it does enable the Spiritual Covering, preventing the enemy from having its way with us. For this reason, we should not fall on grace as an excuse for folly; it only compounds the recompensatory process.

Just so we are clear, the grace and mercy extended to us, covering us in our wrongdoings or shadiness, should not be taken for granted or abused. What is more, it does not negate the correctional, training, or redirection process of governing our Spiritual Astuteness from the inside out; it only prolongs the process. What does this mean? We may wander in our *Desert Experience* longer than we expected until we learn the lessons that need to be learned.

The Temperament of God is not something one would want to joke around with. Why should we not joke around with Him? He is the *Head Chief* in charge. The moment we forget this, we become susceptible to the issues of life or the misguidance of it. If we think our agenda can supersede God's, we are sadly mistaken. Even if we go to the dark side to manipulate the Spiritual System or Divine Order, it is only temporary; thus, it contains an even higher Spiritual Penalty for violating Spiritual Protocols anyway. What is the penalty? It will vary from person to person, but if our waywardness is unjustified or we attempt to outsmart God, pouncing upon one of His Chosen Vessels to prove a point, the penalty is even higher. So, we must be cautious about what or whom we entertain.

Spiritually Calculated or not, we will never know how long the penalty or curse will linger in our Bloodlines, nor do we want to risk it. How does this apply to us? For example, Eve listened to a certain voice of deception, then turned around to coax Adam into doing likewise. Her actions and Adam's lack of correction and obedience before indulging resulted in their being booted out of the Garden of Eden. Bearing this form of Spiritual Negligence created a domino effect in the Bloodline of the human race. And now, here we are! The moral of the story is not to drag others into a mess, even if we feel justified in doing so, or if we are feeling so slick that we can get away with it.

On this note, as we move on, I hear a lot of Spirit-Led individuals saying God told me this, and God told me that. Of course, I am not God, and I cannot discount what they are saying. Still, at the same time, as it relates to the *Spiritual Calculations* of Heaven, I need to know what they are saying to themselves or what the Familiar Spirit is saying.

How is it possible to know the inner chatter of someone, especially when I cannot get into their head? First, without judging, I take note of their character, people skills, approach, reactions, attitude, and Fruits of the Spirit. Secondly, I take note of their body language. Thirdly, the Spirit recognizes and respects Spirit, especially if one is at a certain Level of Spirituality. Therefore, I can determine who is speaking, be it them, the Holy Spirit, or a Familiar Spirit.

In the Realm of the Spirit, one does not need man-made titles to prove Spiritual Authority or Relevance. For example, if I am approached with disrespect, I already know what time it is without uttering one word or proving a point. God is of love, and if hate, abuse, torture, or manipulation is intermingled, it is 'just cause' for me to exercise extreme caution. For what reason would I do so? The Spirit of Deception is lurking about with or without our permission. More importantly, an individual may not be aware of being used as a weapon of deceit. Even if their heart is in the right place, the method of operation is all wrong, according to the Kingdom.

Of course, some things are Divinely Inspired; however, not all that is spoken is from the Heavenly of Heavens. Based upon Spiritual Protocols, Principles, and Laws, we must decipher between truth and lies because deception is always knocking on our door as a form of Light.

Adam and Eve will vouch that deceit will not be packaged as a person, place, or thing we would reject. As a matter of fact, it will cater to an unmet desire, need, fantasy, or want, giving the appearance of what we interpret to be from God when it is not from the Heavenly of Heavens. For this reason, the scriptures tell us, *"Beloved, do not believe every spirit, but test the spirits, whether they are of God; because many false prophets have gone out into the world. By this you know the Spirit of God: Every spirit that confesses that Jesus Christ has come in the flesh is of God, and every spirit that does not confess that Jesus Christ has come in the flesh is not of God. And this is the spirit of the Antichrist, which you have heard was coming, and is now already in the world."* 1 John 4:1-3.

Spiritual Insight and Instincts are desperately needed for such a time as this. When we are desperate, we may find ourselves using alternate means or measures of getting things done. *"For the LORD your God is testing you to know whether you love the LORD your God with all your heart and with all your soul."* Deuteronomy 13:3b. Regardless of how we *Spiritually Calculate* our lives, there will also be conditions in place to protect our Promise. What are the conditions? According to scripture:

- ☐ **The Command**: *"And it shall be that if you earnestly obey My commandments which I command you today, to love the LORD your God and serve Him with all your heart and with all your soul, then I will give you the rain for your land in its season, the early rain and the latter rain, that you may gather in your grain, your new wine, and your oil. And I will send grass in your fields for your livestock, that you may eat and be filled."* Deuteronomy 11:13-15.

- ☐ **The Repercussions**: *"Take heed to yourselves, lest your heart be deceived, and you turn aside and serve other gods and worship them,* lest the LORD's anger be aroused against you, and He shut up the heavens so that there be no rain, and the land yield no produce, and you perish quickly from the good land which the LORD is giving you." Deuteronomy 11:16-17.

☐ **The Preventative Method**: *"Therefore you shall lay up these words of mine in your heart and in your soul, and bind them as a sign on your hand, and they shall be as frontlets between your eyes. You shall teach them to your children, speaking of them when you sit in your house, when you walk by the way, when you lie down, and when you rise up."* Deuteronomy 11:18-19.

☐ **The Executive Method**: *"And you shall write them on the doorposts of your house and on your gates, that your days and the days of your children may be multiplied in the land of which the LORD swore to your fathers to give them, like the days of the heavens above the earth."* Deuteronomy 11:20-21.

☐ **The Reward**: *"For if you carefully keep all these commandments which I command you to do—to love the LORD your God, to walk in all His ways, and to hold fast to Him—then the LORD will drive out all these nations from before you, and you will dispossess greater and mightier nations than yourselves. Every place on which the sole of your foot treads shall be yours: from the wilderness and Lebanon, from the river, the River Euphrates, even to the Western Sea, shall be your territory."* Deuteronomy 11:22-24.

☐ **The Divine Decree**: *"No man shall be able to stand against you; the LORD your God will put the dread of you and the fear of you upon all the land where you tread, just as He has said to you. Behold, I set before you today a blessing and a curse: the blessing, if you obey the commandments of the LORD your God which I command you today; and the curse, if you do not obey the commandments of the LORD your God, but turn aside from the way which I command you today, to go* *after other gods which you have not known."* Deuteronomy 11:25-28.

- ☐ **The Commission**: *"For you will cross over the Jordan and go in to possess the land which the LORD your God is giving you, and you will possess it and dwell in it. And you shall be careful to observe all the statutes and judgments which I set before you today."* Deuteronomy 11:31-32.

If we approach the Promises of God in phases, we are better able to pinpoint our point of error to avoid missing out on our 'best life,' *As It Pleases Him.* In my opinion, it also keeps us from becoming overwhelmed or frustrated with the process while keeping us from overlooking what is best for us in the Sight of God.

The 'good life' and 'best life' are both matters of perception; however, if we are avoiding our Gifting, Calling, Talent, or Mission, we cannot live our 'best life' due to an inner void of missing something. Yet, and still, the illusion of the 'best life' without God can be viewed by those looking from the outside in, through the lenses of deception. However, the one who is living the presumable 'good life' or 'best life' will feel the ALIENATION of the Kingdom from the inside out.

When the glitz and glamour fade or when we are behind closed doors, the truth unveils itself in our habits, thoughts, character, and behaviors. Before we move on, let me ask a few questions, but not limited to such:

- ☐ Do we think our 'best life' is derived from hatefulness, insensitivity, or selfishness?
- ☐ Do we think our 'best life' is derived from unhappiness, unforgiveness, or bitterness?
- ☐ Do we think our 'best life' is derived through chaos, fussing, and fighting?
- ☐ Do we think our 'best life' is derived from impatience, haughtiness, or tardiness?

- ☐ Do we think our 'best life' is derived from unkindness, rudeness, or disrespectfulness?
- ☐ Do we think our 'best life' is derived from bad behavior, folly, or corruption?
- ☐ Do we think our 'best life' is derived from unfaithfulness, player-hating, and deception?
- ☐ Do we think our 'best life' is derived from abrasiveness, hardness, or cruelty?
- ☐ Do we think our 'best life' is derived from the lack of self-control or being all over the place, Mentally, Physically, Emotionally, or Spiritually?
- ☐ Do we think our 'best life' is derived from crucifying others out of jealousy, envy, pride, or covetousness?
- ☐ Do we think our 'best life' is derived from dragging the innocent through the dirt, abusing others, or initiating injustice?
- ☐ Do we think our 'best life' is derived from ruthlessness, anger, or bullying?

Once again, let me say the 'good life' or 'best life' is a matter of perception; however, in the Eye of God, we are held accountable for the life we live in or out of the Kingdom. But there is one thing for sure: We cannot use people, bribe them, or offer kickbacks in Kingdom Matters. We are required to do our part, put in the work for ourselves, and do what we are called to do. Now, if we choose not to do so or digress in this formality, then we cannot place the blame elsewhere.

Even if we are clueless or do not have any apparent help, we have been given the Holy Spirit as a Spiritual Guide to lead us in the ways of the Kingdom; therefore, we have zero excuses for not trying. Well, how do we know if our *Spiritual Calculations* are off? Listed below are a few ways, but not limited to such:

- ☐ When materialism and greed become our driving force, while oppressing others to get what we want.

- When we become co-dependent on the opinions or thoughts of others due to some form of hidden insecurities, as opposed to teaming up with God.
- When we develop a deaf ear to the Ways of God.
- When we are focused on doing our own thing by any means necessary, while leaving a lot of broken or unresolved relationships along the way, without any form of remorse.
- When we operate in fear as opposed to faith.
- When we fall prey to conditioning and biases instigating negative behaviors, thoughts, or judgments.
- When we strive from lies, deception, and chaos.
- When we are quick to point the finger as opposed to assuming responsibility.
- When selfish wants, needs, and desires drive us.
- When we think we have all the answers, while pouncing on those who do not.
- When we are willing to go to the dark side to get what we want.
- When we do not have a clue about our God-Given Mission, Gifting, or Talent.

The *Spiritual Calculations* of the Heavenly of Heavens are not here to deceive us; they are here to enlighten us or illuminate our path without buying into some form of deception. Listen, there is a *Heavenly Manifold* embedded in our DNA, and if we think for a moment God is not in this equation with us, then think again.

Chapter 8

Heavenly Manifold

The *Heavenly Manifold* of God is Divine. In or out of our relational experiences, we must know and understand the Power of the Manifolds and the value hidden in our Spiritual Accountability through earthly measures. As we all know, we are of Earthen Vessels as it relates to our Divine Design; however, for some odd reason, we are falling short in our application process according to the *Spiritual Calculations* from the Heavenly of Heavens. Just so we are clear, this chapter is not written to point the finger at anyone; it is for Spiritual Edification and Divine Revelation.

From God's Perspective, we are all in this Earthly Experience together as One and as our Brother's Keeper. If one has a desire to interject hatefulness into what I am saying, I would suggest that one stop reading right now. If one is not ready for Spiritual Accountability, then it is best to leave the Spiritual Classroom until Spiritual Readiness is established.

Unbeknown to most, the Spiritual Folds of God are prominent in the Kingdom. God gives us all an opportunity, even if we are of another kind. What does this mean? We are all different, with different wants, needs, desires, conditionings, thoughts, and the list goes on. However, when it comes down to our Spiritual Fold, we must set aside our differences and focus on the Voice of God over the voices of ourselves and the people. If we cannot hear God correctly, we are definitely not hearing ourselves or others correctly.

According to the *Spiritual Calculations* of the Heavenly of Heavens, incorrect hearing, speaking, and seeing contribute to how we allow the worldly multiples to work against the Heavenly Singular. What does this mean? Let us begin with the multiplicities of worldliness, but not limited to:

- ☐ Multiple Divides.
- ☐ Multiple Minds.
- ☐ Multiple Bodies.
- ☐ Multiple Vices.
- ☐ Multiple Personalities.
- ☐ Multiple Thoughts.
- ☐ Multiple Voices.
- ☐ Multiple Visions.
- ☐ Multiple Egos.
- ☐ Multiple Religions.
- ☐ Multiple Idols.
- ☐ Multiple gods.

Spiritually, the multiples may be relevant and true; however, it is through the multiples that the enemy gains entry. How is this possible? When we are divided, anything goes. Even if it is not voiced, the soulish realm senses the confusion, causing us to bounce back and forth, leaving an open door for the enemy to sneak in. Lo and behold, the moment we become weak, the possession takes place. Once this happens, if we do not know what to do or if we do not tap into the Oneness of Spirit, we will become tossed around like a little rag doll, not knowing what hit us or where it came from.

For example, when Eve was tempted in the Garden, if she had combated the temptation with the Oneness of God, she could have circumvented her source of entertainment or duality. More importantly, she would not have drawn Adam into her mess when she fell short, and she could have repented of her ignorance. Yet, when she took her ignorance a step further, it meant she knew what she was doing. How is this possible when she is deceived? Deceived or not, the moment she bit into the Forbidden Fruit, the possession had already taken place, provoking the '*Enemy from Within*,' passing it into our Bloodline.

If we take a look at babies, for example, if we place tempting and non-tempting food in front of them, they will naturally gravitate toward the tempting by default. If we do not want them to put it in their mouths, we should not put it in front of them, right? The same principle applies to us as well; this is why we need to exhibit self-control, especially when we lack understanding or know-how.

The moment we fall short, we must know how to repent quickly! Willful weaknesses and divides will happen to us all, yet if we continue to wallow or entertain our vices, it can break our Oneness with God. Therefore, we must stay on high alert, becoming aware of the hidden tricks of the enemy designed to discount who God says we are! Who are we? According to the *Spiritual Calculations* of the Heavenly of Heavens, we are OVERCOMERS, especially when we master the ability to create a win-win out of sin to benefit the Kingdom. What is the purpose of doing so? It builds Kingdom Trust.

Life is a series of lessons, and if we are learners who apply, help, and serve the Kingdom without fail, it increases our Spiritual Ranking and Usability. Most think it is about passing every test. When, in all actuality, it is about how we use and respond to our failed tests. Furthermore, without positive and negative experiences or the woes of life, we will become forgetful, careless, and biased, taking people, places, things, or events for granted without realizing it, especially if it is not documented.

From experience, I am able to write with such passion because I have fallen short and failed many times; yet, through it all, my documentation process became impeccable in the Eye of God. But the key to it all is that I did not stay down regardless of the ridicule, mockery, and judgments of others. With my head held high, I dusted myself off, learned the lesson, and then activated the Law of Reciprocity to share my findings with another to create a win-win. I do not waste lessons; instead, I create a *Heavenly Manifold* to enhance the lives of all those who are willing to glean from the Vestibule of Wisdom.

Although we all have a different story, in the end, the *Spiritual Calculations* of the Heavenly of Heavens are the same. The *Calculations of God* are just, and they do not change. The moment we begin to understand and use them the way they were intended, the Spiritual Formulation of our lives must avail itself, ushering us into our Divine Destiny in the Spirit of Oneness. How is this possible when we are all different? Once again, the *Spiritual Calculations* of the Heavenly of Heavens are Absolute, serving the just and unjust alike.

With the Spiritual Tools hidden in the Hierarchy of Oneness, we have a chance to rewrite our stories, regardless of our past. However, just so we are clear, Oneness does have many Layers of Spirituality similar to the Heavens; nevertheless, we must come to an understanding that our Oneness is orchestrated by the ONE who created it. According to the *Spiritual Calculations* of the Heavenly of Heavens, listed below are a few examples of how Oneness can work on our behalf, but not limited to:

- ☐ One God.
- ☐ One Body.
- ☐ One Mind.
- ☐ One Heart.
- ☐ One Love.
- ☐ One Peace.
- ☐ One Unity.
- ☐ One Flock.
- ☐ One Mission.
- ☐ One Truth.
- ☐ One Faith.
- ☐ One Language.

We can tiptoe around the Oneness that was *Spiritually Calculated* in our DNA, but if the truth is told, it links us all together in some way. How? The underlying DNA of dirt does not change! Dirt is dirt, and if we come from the same place, we are related, period! Besides, the DNA of our Oneness has not changed as well. What does this mean? In scripture, it says, "*So God created man in His own image, in the Image of God He created him; male and female He created them.*" Genesis 1:27. By refuting this, it zaps our Oneness by default. However, all is not lost; the Spiritual Fold is our saving grace to embrace our differences in the Oneness of the Kingdom.

When we can link ourselves and our differences back to the Source for molding, correcting, training, or nurturing, we position ourselves to become usable in the Kingdom from the inside out. How is this possible when our life does not represent the Kingdom? God is looking for willingness, as well as a specific knowing of "*I am the good shepherd; and I know My sheep, and am known by My own. As the Father knows Me, even so I know the Father; and I lay down My life for the sheep. And other sheep I have which are not of this fold; them also I must bring, and they will hear My voice; and there will be one flock and one shepherd.*" John 10:14-16.

A Spiritual Fold is used as a form of protection for Kingdom Builders who are called to Shepherd, cover, and encourage a few types of sheep, but not limited to such:

- ☐ Those who are in waiting or a holding pattern for Divine Purpose.
- ☐ Those who have gone astray or been misled by another.
- ☐ Those who are defiant but usable.
- ☐ Those who are knowingly or unknowingly naive.
- ☐ Those who are misunderstood.
- ☐ Those who are traumatized Mentally, Physically, Emotionally, and Spiritually.
- ☐ Those who have been neglected, ostracized, and abused.
- ☐ Those who are Marked for the Kingdom but not yet ready.
- ☐ Those who are stuck in the mud are in need of a trustworthy hand to pull them out.
- ☐ Those who have failed but are in need of guidance on how to create a win-win.
- ☐ Those who are oblivious to the Word of God.
- ☐ Those who have been deceived.

The *Fold of Man* or the *Man in a Fold* is predicated on the contents of our hearts. What is the big deal about a Spiritual Fold or *Heavenly Manifold*? When we become strong enough to place someone in a Fold, be it Spiritual or not, with no strings attached, our Fold becomes stronger as a result.

Once we become agile enough to withstand the winds of rejection for the Kingdom from the inside out, our *Heavenly Manifold* is unveiled. Just so we are clear, the *Heavenly Manifold* is available to all, yet not all may want to put in the Spiritual Training to get to this Level of Spirituality. Christlike Character, the Fruits of the Spirit, and Accountability are of the utmost precedence in the area of the Holy of Holies. What does this mean for us? Sad but true, God will take us out at the drop of a dime for playing around on Holy Ground; if not Physically, definitely Mentally, Emotionally, and Spiritually.

Regardless of who we are, why we are, or with whom, we do not want to become the enemy of God in any way, shape, or form. He has given us the free will to serve whatever or whomever, but when it comes down to the Spiritual Fold or *Heavenly Manifold*, this is a hands-off zone of Spiritual Sacredness. The bottom line is that if an encroachment is not warranted, we should not play around with fire, especially on Holy or Marked Ground. The fire will consume us and everything we own until the generational curse is reversed or our Bloodline is annihilated.

The punishment seems quite harsh for touching what is Sacred, right? In our eyes, it seems a bit harsh. Yet, Spiritually, if respect is not developed or we attempt to hurt a person God has Spiritually Marked, we will have a problem with Him, or we may become His enemy, period. Frankly, there is NO EXCEPTION to this rule, especially if we are engaging out of spite or due to a bruised ego! Is this Biblical? Of course, it also describes the cause as well. It says, *"Where do wars and fights come from among you? Do they not come from your desires for pleasure that war in your members? You lust and do not have. You murder and covet and cannot obtain. You fight and war. Yet you do not have because you do not ask. You ask and do not receive, because you ask amiss, that you may spend it on your pleasures. Adulterers and adulteresses! Do you not know that friendship with the world is enmity with God? Whoever therefore wants to be a friend of the world makes himself an enemy of God."* James 4:1-4.

How is it possible for God to Spiritually Mark a person? God not only places a Spiritual Mark on people, but He will also place it on a place at His discretion, or He may place it on a thing, such as with the Ark of the Covenant, for various reasons. And if we are not Spiritually Astute, we may become oblivious to the Spiritual Marking, especially if we are Spiritually Blind, Deaf, or Mute.

More importantly, if we do not know how to tap into the Realm of the Spirit, we must exercise extreme caution when engaging in ill will or looming curses out of our mouths. We do not know who possesses the Spiritual Marking from the Heavenly of Heavens, and we can reap fire and brimstones upon our heads or into our Bloodlines! Is this Biblical? I would have it no other way. *"And the Lord said to him, 'Therefore, whoever kills Cain, vengeance shall be taken on him sevenfold.' And the Lord set a MARK on Cain, lest anyone finding him should kill him."* Genesis 4:15. Therefore, we must become ever so careful about what we are doing and the reasons why.

Suppose we do not understand how the Spiritual Elements of the Kingdom work. In this case, we should NOT engage in concocting a plan of contempt to satiate our ego or the ego of another. Let me make a statement from scripture, *"And He said, 'What have you done? The voice of your brother's blood cries out to Me from the ground."* Spiritual Accountability has profound power in the Kingdom, even if we feel exempt from our earthly accounts, regardless of what we are deceived into believing! When we know better and choose not to do better, we are accountable, especially if blood has been shed Mentally, Physically, Emotionally, or Spiritually. Although, as a form of worldly deception, we get locked in on the debauchery of physical bloodshed, from a Spiritual Perspective, we are accountable for the other forms of bloodshed as well.

As it relates to the *Spiritual Calculations* of the Heavenly of Heavens, we must become cautious about what we engage in and with whom. What does this mean? The STAIN of bloodshed does not go away for condoning what could have been prevented until it serves its time in our Bloodline. What about repentance and forgiveness? It is definitely needed and honored by God; however, when our hands are UNJUSTIFIABLY stained with Blood, we have limits in the Kingdom. Really? Yes, really.

For example, God pumped the brakes on David, the man after His own heart. When it came down to building the Temple of the Lord, he could not build it—he was only able to contribute to the cause by setting the *Spiritual Calculations* in place for his son, Solomon. Here is the scripture, "*Now David said, 'Solomon my son is young and inexperienced, and the house to be built for the LORD must be exceedingly magnificent, famous and glorious throughout all countries. I will now make preparation for it.' So David made abundant preparations before his death. Then he called for his son Solomon, and charged him to build a house for the LORD God of Israel. And David said to Solomon: My son, as for me, it was in my mind to build a house to the name of the LORD my God; but the word of the LORD came to me, saying, You have shed much blood and have made great wars; you shall not build a house for My name, because you have shed much blood on the earth in My sight.*" 1 Chronicles 22:5-8. We will also find the Spiritual Commissioning as well as the in-depth *Spiritual Calculations* located in 1 Chronicles 28.

When it comes down to being justified or unjustified, it is of great importance in the Kingdom of Heaven. God is weighing the contents of our hearts as well as our secret or open motives. Therefore, when entering or exiting a Spiritual Fold, we must become crystal clear in our endeavors. More importantly, if we are a Prophet of the Kingdom, we are required to follow Spiritual Protocols, Laws, and Orders while advising accordingly. If not, we are roped into the culpable negligence clause as well.

Once we are Spiritually Appointed, Commissioned, and Positioned as a Prophet of the Kingdom, we are **required** to do a JOB. And if it is not done through the omission process to appease others, if we knowingly whitewash, or if we are not advising of Spiritual Consequences and Repercussions as a preventative method, we are accountable as well. Is this fair? Of course, it is.

God does not require us to fix the problem, pass judgment, or hit someone over the head with the Bible, as most would think; that is God's job. However, in Earthen Vessels, we are required to do a few things, but not limited because each situation may vary:

- ☐ We must understand and state the problem or issue directly or indirectly by asking an open-ended question or sharing a relevant story, provoking one to think or gather information.

- ☐ We must advise the Spiritual Consequences, Laws, or Protocols associated.

- ☐ We must convey why it poses a problem with God or in the Kingdom.

- ☐ We must provide a way out, a point of direction, or a proposed solution.

When it comes down to Kingdom Principalities, our approach is everything. If we approach someone the wrong way, they will boot us out Mentally, Physically, Emotionally, and Spiritually. Now, if they allow us in their personal or headspace, we must master the ability to speak their language without disrespecting them.

We must learn how to maximize the opportunity given without tripping ourselves up or appearing weak as an Ambassador of the Kingdom. Frankly, if respect is lost at this point, things can go to the left; therefore, we cannot put friendly lollygagging over doing what we have been called to do for the Kingdom, *As It Pleases God*. Listed below are a few ways to remain in control of our Spiritual Platform to advise the advisable, but not limited to such:

- ☐ We must master the ability to speak to a person calmly and without aggression or anger.

- ☐ We cannot speak above their head.

- ☐ We must speak on their level of understanding.

- ☐ We cannot leave them hanging.

- ☐ We cannot become gung-ho on pointing out wrongness—we must point out what is right with them as well.

- ☐ We must do our homework to remain *Spiritually Calculated* and Accurate.

- ☐ We must master the ability to ask fact-finding questions or communicate effectively.

- ☐ We must transparently lead by example.

- ☐ We must exhibit the Fruits of the Spirit and Christlike Character.

- ☐ We must master the ability to paint pictures Mentally, Physically, Emotionally, and Spiritually, giving them the ability to follow along with their Mind's Eye.

- ☐ We must be consistent. If we are wishy-washy, it creates doubt and distrust.

- ☐ We must step into the Spiritual Classroom to prepare before presenting while incorporating the Holy Trinity in all things.

Once our job is done, if they turn a deaf ear to us, we are exempt from the culpable negligence clause, and we are free to wash our hands, moving on to the next project.

If we do not know about Spiritual Order, Consequences, Laws, and Repercussions, then with all due respect, we need to step back into the Spiritual Classroom for updates. Listen, the Prophet Nathan did not spare David's feelings, his ego, or his wrath. When David, yes, King David, was out of order, Nathan was instructed to inform him on each occasion. And if we fear man as opposed to God, or if we are celebrating the downfall of our brethren, then we have work to do.

How can we begin to work on ourselves, partaking of the *Heavenly Manifold* of the Kingdom? The best way to do so is to establish an understanding of Spiritual Values from a Kingdom Perspective without interjecting worldliness into the Spiritual Equation. For example, according to the *Spiritual Calculations* of God at the Burning Bush, He did three things before introducing Himself to Moses:

1. He made the call.
2. He established boundaries.
3. He gave instructions.

Here is the scripture, "*So when the LORD saw that he turned aside to look, God called to him from the midst of the bush and said, 'Moses, Moses!' And he said, 'Here I am.' Then He said, 'Do not draw near this place. Take your sandals off your feet, for the place where you stand is holy ground.' Moreover He said, 'I am the God of your father—the God of Abraham, the God of Isaac, and the God of Jacob.' And Moses hid his face, for he was afraid to look upon God.*" Exodus 3:4-6. Why would He give instructions before the introduction? It is done to TEST our Spirit of Obedience. More importantly, when dealing with any type of Spiritual Fold, we must know this: "*My sheep hear My voice, and I know them, and they follow Me.*" John 10:27.

There are times when we recognize the Blessing and miss the Voice of God containing the Spiritual Terms of Use or Decree. Without this, we are left with doubt and disbelief, without getting the 'How-To' in the middle of a Divine Blessing. Why? There are many reasons, but most often, we are still holding on to Spiritual Blindness, Deafness, and Muteness of comfortability.

In or out of a Spiritual Fold, God is not providing a Realm of Comfort—He is provoking a Realm of Awareness. When it is time to move, we are queued up and ready to move at the drop of a dime with the Fruits of the Spirit and *Heavenly Sprinkles* in hand as Soldiers of the Kingdom. Above all, we have our feet shodded, moving forward in the Spirit of Excellence with a *Heavenly Manifold* as our Present Help in our time of need, *As It Pleases God*.

Chapter 9

Heavenly Sprinkles

When the Bible speaks about sprinkles, it is usually referred to as the sprinkling of blood or water on God's Altar for Spiritual Cleansing or Baptism. Although we focus more on Spiritual Baptism, we do not often elaborate on the essence of Spiritual Cleansing. We often do not recognize its relevance or importance in the Kingdom of God. What makes this so important? According to scripture, Jesus said in John 3:5, "*Most assuredly, I say to you, unless one is born of water and the Spirit, he cannot enter the Kingdom of God.* Although this scripture seems very simple, the misinterpretation of it causes us to miss the mark or pray amiss, even when our intentions are right. How is this possible? We focus on being *born of water* (The Baptism), and we totally overlook *the Spirit* (The Spiritual Awakening) aspect of entering the Kingdom.

According to the *Spiritual Calculations* of the Heavenly of Heavens, we need the *Water* and *Spirit*. Why is this the case for Believers? Let me counteract this question with another: 'What is the use of water to cleanse the outside when we are overloaded with filth from within?' The vain repetition of Baptism without the cleansing of our inner parts from the Holy Spirit keeps us bound to worldliness or the dark side of life. Our Spirit, which is lying dormant, must unite as One with the Holy Spirit. If not, we are left to our own devices, be it selfish or worldly.

The Spiritual Relevance of our *Heavenly Sprinkles* has been downplayed, forgotten, or replaced with worldly means of appeasing God or going through the motions for show. When it comes down to the Kingdom, we cannot omit this Spiritual Factor.

Whether we know it or not, the Kingdom of Heaven is at hand. In a world of our own devices, if we choose to play around with Kingdom Principles, we will become caught amid Religion, creating a broader divide within the human psyche, invoking a conscience of debauchery. Is this Biblical? Hebrews 10:22 says, "*Let us draw near with a true heart in full assurance of faith, having our hearts sprinkled from an evil conscience and our bodies washed with pure water.*"

For sure, outer divides represent inner divides, regardless of how we attempt to access them. According to the *Spiritual Calculations* of the Heavenly of Heavens, we are One in the Kingdom, period. Without Oneness, the division is erected among those who are aloof to how the Holy Trinity brings us together as One Body, One Temple, or One Kingdom. As a result, we will fall victim to the Vicissitudes of Life while not gaining Spiritual Access to our *Heavenly Sprinkles* of Divine Liberation.

Religiosity has become one of man's greatest downfalls in today's time. We have forgotten about our Relational Obligations. Our obligations are hidden in our *Spirit to Spirit* Relationship with the Holy Trinity. And, being that Jesus has become the Sacrificial Lamb of God for our sake, we dare not forget!

Why should we remember? First, we are now able to use the *Heavenly Sprinkles* to anoint ourselves, our altar, our lives, our Purposes, our Passions, or anything. Secondly, we have the presence of the Holy Spirit to guide, correct, teach, and provide us with on-the-spot or on-the-job training in the Ways of the Kingdom, *As It Pleases God*. Thirdly, we all need help in bringing forth our Gifts, Calling, Talent, and Purpose or creating a pathway of Breadcrumbs leading ourselves and others into Divine Destiny.

The *Sprinkles of Heaven* is what gives us the ultimate sparkle, leaving a positive imprint on the hearts of all we come in contact with, regardless of what type of picture they choose to paint. How is this possible? If we dare to understand this one scripture about the power encapsulated in our *Heavenly Sprinkles*, we will never doubt whether or not the Kingdom of Heaven really exists. Here is the binding Spiritual Decree, "*For if the blood of bulls and goats and the ashes of a heifer, sprinkling the unclean, sanctifies for the purifying of the flesh, how much more shall the blood of Christ, who through the eternal Spirit offered Himself without spot to God, cleanse your conscience from dead works to serve the living God? And for this reason He is the Mediator of the new covenant, by means of death, for the redemption of the transgressions under the first covenant, that those who are called may receive the promise of the eternal inheritance.*" Hebrews 9:13-15.

Why are the *Heavenly Sprinkles* so important in the Eye of God? Let me share another Spiritual Decree: "*Therefore say to the house of Israel, Thus says the Lord GOD: 'I do not do this for your sake, O house of Israel, but for My holy name's sake, which you have profaned among the nations wherever you went. And I will sanctify My great name, which has been profaned among the nations, which you have profaned in their midst; and the nations shall know that I am the LORD,' says the Lord GOD, 'when I am hallowed in you before their eyes.' For I will take you from among the nations, gather you out of all countries, and bring you into your own land. Then I will sprinkle clean water on you, and you shall be clean; I will cleanse you from all your filthiness and from all your idols. I will give you a new heart and put a new spirit within you; I will take the heart of stone out of your flesh and give you a heart of flesh. I will put My Spirit within you and cause you to walk in My statutes, and you will keep My judgments and do them. Then you shall dwell in the land that I gave to your fathers; you shall be My people, and I will be your God. I will deliver you from all your uncleannesses. I will call for the grain and multiply it, and bring no famine upon you. And I will multiply the fruit of your trees and the increase of your fields, so that you need never again bear the reproach of famine among the nations.*" Ezekiel 36:22-30.

Before we move on, the ones who possess the *Heavenly Sprinkles* of Kingdom Credentials will never appear as such to the naked eye. Their words are often taken for granted until it is too late, and they are often ignored because they are misunderstood. Frankly, this is similar to how Goliath underestimates David due to his size, while at the same time, his brothers, King Saul, and his soldiers misjudged him as well. Why would they underestimate David when they did not dare to contend with Goliath? In my opinion, size, status, and occupation usually do the trick, causing us to judge what or whom we do not understand.

Meanwhile, in the Kingdom, God will use anything or anyone to get the job done. Still, more importantly, it takes a Spiritual Eye to see, a Spiritual Ear to hear, and a Spiritual Tongue to speak under the Authority of the Kingdom. For this reason, those possessing authentic Kingdom Credentials are thoroughly trained, tested, provoked, and corrected before they are commissioned.

Spiritually Speaking, if one has not gone through the Spiritual Battles or possesses the Battle Scars, they are still in the Spiritual Classroom to become equipped to use the Spiritual Tools of the Kingdom. Why are we battling? Then again, why do Believers possess the Battle Scars? First and foremost, we all have Battle Scars, hidden under layers of trauma, conditioning, or biases. Secondly, contending with the enemy is no joke! As Spiritual Beings having a human experience, by the grace of God, those who are WILLING are thoroughly trained and prepared to deal with the enemy's wiles, *As It Pleases Him*.

If we have not conquered the enemy from within, or we are unequipped to use the Whole Armor of God, the Kingdom is required to train us properly. What is the purpose of doing so? It helps to avoid getting innocent people hurt, especially when our Kingdom Experiences are not up to par, or our condemnatory factors are keeled. As a result, Kingdom Thoroughness is required for those bearing Kingdom Credentials. What is the reason for such thoroughness? In or out of the Kingdom, there are many reasons depending upon our Spiritual Mission or Astuteness; however, listed below are a few reasons, but not limited to such:

- ☐ We must become the Holy Temple possessing the Holy Furnishings (the Ark, the Fruits of the Spirit, and Christlike Character) from within, worshipping God in Spirit and in Truth while becoming the Earthly Vessel and Footstool of the Kingdom.

- ☐ We must hear the Voice of God clearly while filtering out the distractions, grabbing the hidden lessons, and continually developing and mastering the Spiritual Language of the Kingdom from the inside out.

- ☐ We must set a Spiritual Guard over our Mind, Body, Soul, and Spirit while staying on high alert for any form of Spiritual Intrusion, knowing how to break it at the drop of a dime.

- ☐ We must put aside our personal issues to do Kingdom Business with clean hands, pure hearts, and a made-up mind to receive the undisputed Spirit of Wisdom while using the Holy Trinity (The Father, Son, and Holy Spirit) as our point of Spiritual Leverage.

- ☐ We must see the enemy in plain sight without allowing them to know their cover is blown while being fervently equipped with the Whole Armor of God, ready to go into Spiritual Combat at the drop of a dime.

- ☐ We must take rejection with a smile on our faces without losing our sense of peace.

- ☐ We will be misunderstood, and we must stand up for the Mission of the Kingdom without fail and without bowing down or abandoning the cause.

- ☐ We must handle loneliness in a state of peace while still possessing powerful people skills and drawing crowds.

- ☐ We must read, write, pray, fast, and study to stay ahead of the game of life. Frankly, if we do not read, write, pray, fast, and study, we will get left behind, being in awe of those who do.

- We must master the ability to cancel negatives while replacing them with positivity, Biblical Scriptures, and positive affirmations to sustain and maintain a Positive Mindset or create a win-win.

- We must be consistent without allowing doubt to invade our Gifts, Callings, Talents, or Purposes. Plus, we cannot create an overkill illusion of being more than we are to impress others while humbly walking in the Mission of the Kingdom despite naysayers, setbacks, or perilous conditions.

- We must understand beyond a shadow of a doubt that everyone is a work in progress. What is more, we must become highly sensitive to our faults and misbehaviors, assuming responsibility, repenting quickly, and sincerely working on becoming better. Why is this necessary for Believers? To avoid the Rod of Correction from bringing about a heavy Spiritual Lashing or Shame to our names.

The fascinating part about God is that we are all the *'Apple of God's Eye'* until we prove Him otherwise, or we turn our backs on him once we get what we want. But, in order to become *Heavenly Sprinkles* of the Kingdom, we must put in the work. God will not move Heaven and Earth for us when we will not lift a finger for Him, His sheep, or the Kingdom.

Now, according to the *Spiritual Calculations* of the Heavenly of Heavens, selfishness, pompousness, disobedience, or the lack of humility get us booted out of the Kingdom Benefits, similar to what happened to Saul in 1 Samuel. What did he do? At first, when he was not the King, he operated in humility and obedience. What is more, Samuel explained the behaviors associated with Royalty in the Kingdom in 1 Samuel 10:25. Yet, once Saul got a little taste of power, he became a few things:

- Foolish.

- ☐ Rebellious.
- ☐ Disobedient.
- ☐ Jealous.
- ☐ Envious.
- ☐ Prideful.
- ☐ Cruel.
- ☐ Rude.
- ☐ Reckless in his actions, reactions, and demeanor.
- ☐ Abusing his power.
- ☐ Levying unwarranted curses.
- ☐ A lover of himself.

In Saul's reign, the straw that broke the camel's back was the moment he consulted a witch in 1 Samuel 28, invoking the Prophet Samuel, who was already dead. In my opinion, this is like slapping God in the face. How? It is an insult to God to consult the dead or go to the dark side regarding the living, especially when he was outright trying to kill David, the next King in line and God's Chosen Elect. What is the big deal? He was already his own enemy from within, but when he attempted to kill or curse what or whom God had Spiritually Anointed, he became the Enemy of God.

Sadly, Saul possessed a dark soul of contradiction. How? First, God took him from a donkey herder to a king, and he willingly threw the Spirit of the Lord away for selfish reasons. Secondly, when the Prophet Samuel was still living and on his side, he would not listen, turning away from God to do his own thing. Thirdly, he had the audacity to go to the dark side for Divine Revelation, especially when the Prophet Samuel had already given him the behaviors associated with the Royalty of the Kingdom in writing. After outright rejecting God, now he wants to listen! What an insult to the Kingdom, right?

The truth of the matter is that Saul had Spiritual Access, not realizing the power he had until it was gone, while trying to kill another man for doing what he chose not to do. What was he not willing to do? He was not willing to obey, repent, and do the right thing in the Sight of God or *As It Pleased Him.*

Now, according to the *Spiritual Calculations* of the Heavenly of Heavens, the Spirit of the Lord cannot remain in chaos and disobedience. Rule number one: If we cannot tolerate being corrected, we will be rejected in the Kingdom. Just so we are clear, God loves us all; yet, when it comes down to Kingdom Access, we have Rules of Royalty, and if one cannot obey, they cannot stay!

The *Heavenly Sprinkles* of the Kingdom does not require perfection; it involves the work-in-progress mentality, giving an attentive ear to our Spiritual Mentor, Teacher, or Prophet. If Saul had listened to the Spiritual Mentor that God had Blessed him with, he would not have negatively turned on God, himself, or others.

Listen, when we become the Enemy of God, we inadvertently become an enemy to ourselves from the inside out. What does this mean? We will secretly or openly turn on ourselves while blaming others for our inability to take responsibility for our actions, reactions, thoughts, desires, or whatever, creating another '*Garden of Eden*' experience of being banished from the Kingdom.

Now, if we have a desire to flip the script on any form of banishment, we need a few Kingdom Principles under our belt working on our behalf. Is this Biblical? Let us take it to scripture: "*Thus says the Lord GOD: On the day that I cleanse you from all your iniquities, I will also enable you to dwell in the cities, and the ruins shall be rebuilt. The desolate land shall be tilled instead of lying desolate in the sight of all who pass by. So they will say, 'This land that was desolate has become like the Garden of Eden; and the wasted, desolate, and ruined cities are now fortified and inhabited.' Then the nations which are left all around you shall know that I, the LORD, have rebuilt the ruined places and planted what was desolate. I, the LORD, have spoken it, and I will do it. Thus says the Lord GOD: 'I will also let the house of Israel inquire of Me to do this for them: I will increase their men like a flock. Like a flock offered as holy sacrifices, like the flock at Jerusalem on its feast days, so shall the ruined cities be filled with flocks of men. Then they shall know that I am the LORD.*" Ezekiel 36:33-38.

For the record, King David was not a saint by any means, yet he was after God's own heart. Now the question is, 'How did David become after God's own heart?' First, he became a Servant, leading God's sheep under the designated Spiritual Covenant set in place, *As It Pleased Him*. Secondly, he was quick to pray, forgive, repent, and fast about any and everything. Thirdly, he listened to his Spiritual Teacher, Advisor, Mentor, or whatever. Fourthly, he did not attempt to kill someone he knew was anointed by God. But just so we are clear, if God told him to take someone out, they were as 'good as gone' without him batting an eye.

Although David was prevented from doing certain things for the Kingdom for having too much blood on his hands and misusing his authority to kill Uriah, it did not stop God from using him in a mighty way. David operated in Kingdom Principles with no regrets, passing the Spiritual Wisdom to his son Solomon, the wisest man according to scripture. Spiritually, Solomon's mother, Bathsheba, played a vital role in the transfer of wisdom, but with all due respect, his daddy was the anchor in God's heart.

Now, according to the *Spiritual Calculations* of the Heavenly of Heavens, in order to lead God's sheep effectively, one must become mentored by God himself or a Shepherd after God's own heart. The Spiritual Classroom of Kingdom Principles is mandatory for the Spirit of Wisdom to rest or reside from within.

How can we obtain the same level of Spiritual Wisdom? For starters, the Book of Psalms and Proverbs will help us. And then, we must master the ability to use Kingdom Principles consistently and effectively. Once done, the rest will take care of itself, even if it feels as if someone is spitting in our faces or they are royally using us.

In the Eye of God, our enemies, the naysayers, or the dream killers make the best platforms or footstools for us, giving us the ability to forgive, extend mercy, avoid provocations, control our emotions, redirect our thoughts, and maximize our greatest potential. All we need to do is avoid becoming our own enemy, the Enemy of God, or the enemy that must provide the footstool of restitution.

When we are able to keep a straight face, control our emotions, and be kind, loving, and caring at the same time, we are well on our way to mastering our *Heavenly Sprinkles*. How is this possible? What we give comes back in full circle as the Law of Reciprocity stands in full effect. Now, if we do not know this Spiritual Law, we will settle for defeat, settling for whatever life throws at us. However, one must know this Spiritual Law beyond a shadow of a doubt. According to the *Spiritual Calculations* of the Heavenly of Heavens, if we remain in good standing in the Kingdom, this Spiritual Law must fulfill itself based upon the Biblical Law of Seedtime and Harvest. Just keep in mind this Divine Law works positively and negatively, so we must exercise extreme caution.

Our Heavenly Treasures are not engulfed in the big things we brag about; they are encapsulated in the little things we do without bragging. Here is how I break down the Heavenly Treasures of responsibility into *Heavenly Sprinkles*, but not limited to such:

- ☐ When we exhibit Christlike Character, we do not need to brag about being Kind—it is a responsibility to the Kingdom of Heaven.

- ☐ When we exhibit Love, we do not need to brag about Loving God, ourselves, others, or the life we live—it is a responsibility to the Kingdom of Heaven.

- ☐ When we exhibit Joy, we do not need to brag about being Joyous from within—it is a responsibility to the Kingdom of Heaven.

- ☐ When we exhibit Peace, we do not need to brag about being at Peace with God, ourselves, or others—it is a responsibility to the Kingdom of Heaven, and being a hellion on wheels is not of God.

- ☐ When we exhibit Patience, we do not need to brag about being Patient with God, ourselves, or others—it is a responsibility to the Kingdom of Heaven.

- [ ] When we exhibit Kindness, we do not need to brag about being Kind, just be Kind, period. Besides, it is a responsibility to the Kingdom of Heaven.

- [ ] When we exhibit Goodness, we do not need to brag about being or doing Good—it is a responsibility to the Kingdom of Heaven.

- [ ] When we exhibit Faithfulness, we do not need to brag about being Faithful—it is a responsibility to the Kingdom of Heaven.

- [ ] When we exhibit Gentleness, we do not need to brag about being Gentle—it is a responsibility to the Kingdom of Heaven.

- [ ] When we exhibit Self-Control, we do not need to brag about being in control of ourselves—it is a responsibility to the Kingdom of Heaven.

- [ ] When we exhibit Forgiveness, we do not need to brag about Forgiving. In the Eye of God, it is a safeguard for our Mind, Body, Soul, and Spirit. In addition, it is also a responsibility to the Kingdom of Heaven as well.

- [ ] When we exhibit Mercy, we do not need to brag about being Merciful because we are going to need it at some point in our lives as well. More importantly, it is a responsibility to the Kingdom of Heaven.

We can tiptoe around what is or is not expected from us and our responsibilities in or out of the Kingdom of God. Nonetheless, the *Royal Principles* are already written on the Tablet of our Hearts. We only need to learn how to use and master them. So, the moment we think we are fooling God, we are only fooling ourselves instead.

We are equipped with everything we need. We simply need to come to an understanding of our Divine Design or Predestined Blueprint through *Spiritual Dephasing*. And then, use the Spiritual Tools to tap into the *Heavenly Sprinkles* of the *Spiritual Calculations* set in motion from the BEGINNING of time to the End, but accessible right NOW, *As It Pleases God*.

Chapter 10

Spiritual Dephasing

The moment it comes down to the *Spiritual Calculations* of the Heavenly of Heavens, all things are divided as One. This seems like a contradiction, right? Absolutely! God has designed it this way to open us up to all things Spiritual. What does this mean? If we overlook the Source, we may miss the Divine Message or Mission of our Oneness. For example:

- ☐ There is One God, phased as Three Persons (The Father, Son, and Holy Spirit).

- ☐ The Bible is One, phased of many books, chapters, and sections.

- ☐ The Body is One, a phased of many members.

- ☐ The Earth is One, phased of several Continents and bodies of water, divided accordingly.

- ☐ There is One Language of the Kingdom, phased with duality based upon our point of origin.

The Spiritual Classroom is needed to differentiate the Mindset of Oneness or worldliness. Most often, we are led to believe that Spirituality just happens. But the question is, if we are not well-versed in Spirituality, how do we know when it happens? Anyone can learn a few scriptures, and anyone can learn about Spirituality, but not many understand or really experience it, *As It Pleases God*.

How can we not experience Spirituality and be Believers simultaneously? We can be both. Even though we are Spiritual Beings having a human experience, we must understand Spirituality, *As It Pleases God*. If not, we are left to our own interpretations of all things Spiritual. Unfortunately, this is how we get God all wrong, trying to bribe or pimp Him, or begging for things unpleasing to Him. For these reasons, we cannot gain or lose Spiritual Power and Authority in the Eye of God.

Then again, on the other hand, Spirituality is fearful for those who have never experienced true Spirituality, which often results in some form of disbelief. Above all, when dealing with the Ancient of Days, our Spirituality has LEVELS and RANKINGS. If one is clueless about this or operating outside of it, they have not been Spiritually Commissioned from the Kingdom. What does this mean? Spiritual Training is required, period. Just so we are clear, this does not exempt us from experiencing a relationship with God; it merely limits our Spiritual Useability, Divine Wisdom and Secrets, or Access to the Kingdom of Heaven, and it may pump the brakes on our maximum capacity in the use of our Gifts, Calling, Talents, Creativity, or Purpose.

According to the *Spiritual Calculations* of the Heavenly of Heavens, Spirituality is developed. The Laws of the Spirit are Absolute, and anything valuable has debris covering it, similar to a diamond. The debris covering the diamond must be removed to expose the hidden value.

With all due respect, what we equate as being Spiritual may not be. It could come from ourselves, our own interpretations, or conditioning, especially when we do not understand the Spirit Realm. Frankly, with the Kingdom of Heaven, God expects more from us, especially when it comes down to our perception.

When we are going through a phase in our lives, our perception is locked into that moment with a *'pending status.'* What does this mean? Depending upon our situation, conditioning, mindset, or biases, it will determine where we are in life and why. When we are in a *'pending status,'* we will begin to feel our way through life based on our senses, traumas, and unrestrained lusts. Just so we are clear, no one is exempt from this phase; it is just that some learn, some remain, some become yoked, and some become clueless at this moment.

The *Spiritual Dephasing* process can be positive or negative, depending upon our perceptions and willingness. However, from a Spiritual Perspective, it aids in creating the *Heavenly Sprinkles* needed for the Spiritual Propelling Process, *As It Pleases God*.

What is *Spiritual Dephasing*? It is the process of dividing the old self from the new, preventing us from relapsing back to the old by giving us a Spiritually Reformed way of thinking, doing, saying, and becoming. If we do not separate ourselves from worldly ways, we will graft it into the Spiritual while thinking it is right in our own eyes, thwarting our Spiritual Alignment to please ourselves.

For example, the 'Ark of the Covenant' was a *Spiritual Dephasing* Process for the Children of Israel, separating them from the worldliness of the Egyptian mindset or methods of operation. When they thought Moses had died, and due to their lack of faith in God Almighty, they built a golden calf to worship, similar to the Egyptian culture. Not realizing that Moses was on his way back with the Ten Commandments to guide them. What made them do this? They became a victim of the reversion process as opposed to Spiritual Conversion. In life, we have two options:

- ☐ Revert back.
- ☐ Go forward.

What happened to stay the same? According to the *Spiritual Calculations* of the Heavenly of Heavens and the Cycle of Life, we are designed to grow, period. If we do not grow, we will suffer some form of death, Mentally, Physically, Emotionally, or Spiritually, reverting backward instead of forward, similar to the Children of Israel. The truth is that only God remains the same yesterday, today, and forever. If we do not jump on the Bandwagon of Spirituality, we become susceptible to the opposing forces of the Cycle of Life while trapped in time, taking one step forward and two steps back.

More importantly, the moment we feel trapped by something or someone, we symbolically create a life of boulders, knocking ourselves and others to and fro instead of creating *Heavenly Sprinkles*, satiating the hidden thirst of all we come in contact with.

Is it possible to satiate a thirst without knowing the need first? Absolutely! When we lead by example, mastering the *Spiritual Dephasing* Process, we do not have to know the needs of another when we exhibit the Fruits of the Spirit.

According to the *Spiritual Calculations* of the Heavenly of Heavens, we must do a few things to *Spiritually Dephase* ourselves, but not limited to such:

- ☐ We must Decriminalize ourselves.
- ☐ We must De-Lust ourselves.
- ☐ We must De-Materialize ourselves.
- ☐ We must De-Idolize ourselves.
- ☐ We must De-Pride ourselves.
- ☐ We must De-Flesh ourselves.
- ☐ We must Demote ourselves.
- ☐ We must De-Platform ourselves.
- ☐ We must De-Socialize ourselves.
- ☐ We must De-Think ourselves.
- ☐ We must De-Language ourselves.
- ☐ We must De-Vision ourselves.

Why do we need to go through this process? According to the *Spiritual Calculations* of the Heavenly of Heavens, this reformation process helps us to get ourselves out of the way, putting our worldliness at bay. What does this mean? Our soulish nature is the driving force leading us away from the Kingdom and the Truth, whereas our Spirit leads us toward them. If we do not become Spirit-Led, we will miss the mark. In all simplicity, our motives will not match the Motives of God, *As It Pleases Him*, only to please ourselves instead. It is like two worlds colliding, seeking dominance without us realizing the 'I AM' is greater in the Spiritual Equation.

Equating God in all things is Wisdom at its best. It keeps the Spiritual Streaming process flowing toward us instead of away from us. If we avail ourselves to *Spiritual Dephasing*, it helps us in many ways, such as, but not limited to:

- ☐ It helps our Spiritual Fruits to remain fruitful while granting us consistency in their use.

- ☐ It gives us the Mind of Christ, helping us to think Kingdom Thoughts as opposed to worldly ones.

- ☐ It encourages us to exhibit Christlike Character while nudging us when we get out of character.

- ☐ It aids us in becoming and remaining humble while maintaining our inner strength to move forward in confidence.

- ☐ It grants us the 'know-how' or the 'how-to' of moving forward with no regrets.

- ☐ It provides us with the ability to bounce back regardless of how life seems.

- ☐ It contributes to us staying focused even when we are sidetracked or blindsided.

- ☐ It offers peace amid chaos, provocation, and confusion.

- ☐ It pinpoints, narrowing down the root of our issues, problems, setbacks, traumas, or whatever.

- ☐ It puts a line between good and evil, right and wrong, or positive and negative, allowing us to determine the difference.

- ☐ It takes our faith, converting it into reality in due time or when the timing is right.

- ☐ It extends a Spiritual Compass as a focal point, guiding us to the Light through our darkest moments.

The 'Follow the Light' or 'Stay in the Light' mentality works for all who are committed to having a Positive Mental Attitude while creating a win-win out of everything or with anyone. What does the Light have to do with us? According to 1 John 1:17, "*But if we walk in the light as He is in the light, we have fellowship with one another, and the Blood of Jesus Christ His Son cleanses us from all sin.*"

The Covenantal Covering of Light makes us Spiritually Supercharged, similar to the '*Ark of the Covenant*.' Whether we seek the Light or the Covenant, we should not play around with them, nor should we play around with those who possess Kingdom Credentials. How do we know who possesses Kingdom Credentials? We will not know unless the Spirit of God reveals their identity to us. So, we can only speculate outside of a *Spirit to Spirit* encounter or Spiritual Discernment, *As It Pleases God*.

What does the '*Ark of the Covenant*' have to do with us or our *Spiritual Dephasing* Process? First, it is a symbolic reference of the *Spiritual Calculations* of the Heavenly of Heavens, bridging the gap for us to possess Kingdom Credentials by expunging darkness. Secondly, it is our hidden Spiritual Compass guiding us to the Light in Earthen Vessel, heightening our Spiritual Senses and Instincts. Yet, many of us are intrigued about who has the Ark or its location, but from a Spiritual Perspective, we must begin to look for the '*Ark of the Covenant*' from within. God has hidden the '*Garden of Eden*' within us, and He has also hidden the '*Ark of the Covenant*' within us as well.

Listen, all of the *Spiritual Calculations* from the Beginning to the End are already. They are hidden in plain sight from within each and every one of us, and if we do not understand our Temple, we are going to miss out, we are going to miss our cue, and we are going to unintentionally pray amiss. Why are we at such risk as Believers having free will? We need Spiritual Counsel to understand the Elements of the Spirit.

Once again, everything I am speaking about, we already know it—we have simply forgotten that we do. The moment we come to ourselves, *As It Pleases God*, we can better remember what is already. Suppose we embrace our Temple as we protect the 'Ark of the Covenant' by using the Fruits of the Spirit, Christlike Character, and Spiritual Principles, similar to what is explained in the Book of Exodus. In this case, we will find that the Heavens will open up for us. How is this possible? The *Spiritual Calculations* of the Heavenly of Heavens are already built into the Fruits of the Spirit. Frankly, it is similar to how the Fruits of the Spirit are naturally built into the Ten Commandments as well. Is this just a coincidence? Absolutely not.

According to the *Spiritual Calculations* of the Heavenly of Heavens, first and foremost, the Ten Commandments teach us how to relate to God in the top four Commandments and how to deal with people in the latter six. Why were they created in such a manner? It creates Spiritual Order.

Without having Spiritual or Divine Order, our *Spiritual Calculations* will be off every single time due to our self-induced calculations. What does this mean? Worldly motives without God create divides, malice, and disobedience. It also means that we can do the right things for the wrong reasons or at the wrong time, and the wrong things for the right reasons and at the right time. The bottom line is that we need Spiritual help, period!

As the Children of Israel needed Spiritual Guidance for their journey, so do we. In essence, if we want the *'Ark of the Covenant'* Spiritual Decree, we must heed Exodus 23:20-23: *"I am sending an Angel before you to keep you in the way and to bring you into the place which I have prepared. Beware of Him and obey His voice; do not provoke Him, for He will not pardon your transgressions; for My name is in Him. But if you indeed obey His voice and do all that I speak, then I will be an enemy to your enemies and an adversary to your adversaries."*

Will God really protect us in such a manner? Absolutely. The *Rules of Royalty* are not something to joke around with; they are designed to protect what belongs to the Kingdom of God wholeheartedly. So, whatever you need to *Spiritually Dephase*, dephase it now!

Chapter 11

Rules of Royalty

From Genesis to Revelation, disobedience has plagued us and our relationship with God, then spilling over into our people skills with a slanted twist of worldliness, godliness, and selfishness. As a result, it has created a melting pot of disloyalty gone absolutely wrong, while in our eyes, we think we are totally right. For this reason, it is time to draw a line in the sand with our self-aggrandizing rules to create the primal Heaven on Earth Experience as God intended. How is this possible? We are going to digress in our worldly formality to progress in the formal *Rules of Royalty* of the Kingdom of Heaven. What will this do for us? We will become Spiritually Awakened. The moment we come to ourselves, knowing what we believe and why, the 'How-To' will take care of itself with a Spiritual Compass (The Holy Spirit) guiding us to the Light.

According to the *Spiritual Calculations* of the Heavenly of Heavens, *Royalty in the Kingdom* equates to Spiritual Loyalty and Respect in and with our Earthly Experiences. Often, when questioned about loyalty, we will not admit to any form of disloyalty, only to judge and point the finger at another for theirs. What is more, we are quick to embrace the illusion of loyalty to God, even when our hand is in the cookie jar.

Just so we are clear, our loyalty to God is not what is in question according to the *Rules of Royalty*; it is how loyal we are to our people skills. If we are unable to treat people with ordinary dignity and respect, then when it comes down to the Kingdom, nothing changes. The contents of our hearts reveal all, especially regarding our ethics or conduct toward God's Divine Creation. What does this mean? If we cannot get it right here on Earth, we will not get it right in Heaven.

As a result of our secret disloyalty from the inside out, we become reckless with any form of power or authority by default. In the Eye of God, this inner quirk of abuse and mismanagement is often revealed when those who think they have the Spiritual Authority to loom unwarranted curses over the lives of others. Unfortunately, this often happens when a person does not get what they want or when they cannot control something or someone.

In addition, they also engage in hitting people over the head with the Bible, judging others, negatively looking down on people, or equating a person's worth with their own perception, conditioning, biases, or traumas, all in the Name of God. When, in all actuality, this is not God! Nor is this how He operates in the Kingdom. Yet, all is not lost; we can reverse the effects of our ordinary loyalty or disloyalty by becoming Spiritually Equipped with the vital information and *Spiritual Calculations* from the Heavenly of Heavens, *As It Pleases God*.

The Heaven on Earth Experience is not for the faint of heart. Why not? 'Doubt is out' in the Kingdom. When representing the Kingdom, we cannot bounce all over the place, Mentally, Physically, Emotionally, and Spiritually. From my perspective, it is a 'No-Bounce Zone.' When we are Spiritually Commissioned from the Heavenly of Heavens, we are automatically under attack. If we are bound by wavering faith, the bullseye will become centered on our Mind, Body, and Soul, and if our Spirit is not strong enough to withstand the wiles of the enemy or if we do not know how to use the Whole Armor of God, we will be royally crushed.

If we desire to become understood, we must begin to understand God, ourselves, and others. By far, this does not mean that we must agree, but an understanding and respect must be established. God will be God, we will be who we are, and people will be who they are. Why should we violate the free will of another in our Commission of Life? And, if we do not like the Will of God, we have a choice to obey or not to obey.

The best thing about the Kingdom of Heaven is that it has established the *Rules of Royalty* of free will. Now, if we decide to use the *Rules of Royalty* along with our Spiritual Compass, we can become one of the Spiritual Elites in the Kingdom. Really? Yes, really! The *Spiritual Calculations* of our Blessings have a Divine Layout or Blueprint. Suppose we tap into the Kingdom Mentality, giving God what He wants and expects from us. In this case, He will not withhold the information, guidance, or instructions needed to unveil the Secrets of the Heavenly of Heavens.

In the Kingdom, why do we need rules? If we take a moment to experiment with our thoughts, we will find that if they are not guarded, our mind will create anything it wants, whether it is true, false, or indifferent. As it relates to the *Spiritual Calculations* of the Heavenly of Heavens, we must recognize and respect the Power of the Mind, as well as its influences over truths and untruths of God, the Kingdom, ourselves, others, and life in itself.

The *Rules of Royalty* want us to understand that our Mind is a Spiritual Tool and a Gateway to the relational capacity of our Spirituality, Creativity, or the downfall of the human psyche. Our life is predicated on the Root of our Perception filtered through our human senses. If the signal to our perception is mangled, our senses will likewise be mangled.

Suppose we lock our perception on Kingdom Principles, getting the Holy Trinity involved in everything while using the Fruits of the Spirit and Christlike Character. In this case, it changes the rules of the game. As a result, our human senses will become backed up or supported by our Spiritual Instincts by default. How is this possible? The *Spiritual Calculations* of our 'then' and 'now' are wrapped in our perception. If we do not have a Spiritual Buffer in place, they become negative triggers as opposed to positive place markers, letting us know the people, places, and things to avoid or what and whom to entertain with reason.

The *Rules of Royalty* are profound to the Kingdom of Heaven, and God's Chosen Elect must abide to reside. There is a Golden Rule that applies to any kingdom: "*Every kingdom divided against itself is* brought to desolation, and every city or house divided against itself will not stand." Matthew 12:25. Even Satan will not divide his kingdom for us. Is this Biblical? Of course, it says, "If Satan casts out Satan, he is divided against himself. How then will his kingdom stand?" Matthew 12:26. Now, if for some reason we are willfully dividing ourselves, we still have hope.

The Holy Spirit is available to quicken our Spirit to become One with Him as long as we do not commit the Unpardonable Act. What is UNPARDONABLE with the Holy Spirit? As long as we do not blaspheme against the Holy Spirit, we can seek forgiveness; however, if we commit blasphemy against the Holy Spirit, it is unpardonable in the Kingdom of Heaven. Here is what we need to know: *"Therefore I say to you, every sin and blasphemy will be forgiven men, but the blasphemy against the Spirit will not be forgiven men. Anyone who speaks a word against the Son of Man, it will be forgiven him; but whoever speaks against the Holy Spirit, it will not be forgiven him, either in this age or in the age to come."* Matthew 12:31-32.

For the sake of the Kingdom, we must become aware of the *Rules of Royalty* to ensure we do not unawaringly violate them. A tree is known by its fruits, regardless of our characterization, classification, or rationalization in the Kingdom of Heaven. Now, before we go any further, here is why we need to know the *Rules of Royalty*: *"Either make the tree good and its fruit good, or else make the tree bad and its fruit bad; for a tree is known by its fruit. Brood of vipers! How can you, being evil, speak good things? For out of the abundance of the heart the mouth speaks. A good man out of the good treasure of his heart brings forth good things, and an evil man out of the evil treasure brings forth evil things. But I say to you that for every idle word men may speak, they will give account of it in the Day of Judgment. For by your words you will be justified, and by your words you will be condemned."* Matthew 12:33-37.

In today's day and age, we are asking for a sign regarding something or someone, when in all actuality, God wants us to pay attention to the fruits. Our mindset, conditioning, biases, and perceptions can deceive us, whereas the fruits will not. We simply must learn how to recognize them without whitewashing the most evident Declarations of Divine Revelation.

Of course, no one is perfect, but our good fruits must outweigh the bad. While at the same time, using the Fruits of the Spirit and Christlike Character to balance ourselves from the inside out. If we focus on balancing ourselves from the outside in, we will violate Divine Order. How is this possible when we have a choice to live our lives how we desire? According to scripture, it says, *"Come now, you who say, today or tomorrow we will go to such and such a city, spend a year there, buy and sell, and make a profit; whereas you do not know what will happen tomorrow. For what is your life? It is even a vapor that appears for a little time and then vanishes away. Instead you ought to say, 'If the Lord wills, we shall live and do this or that. But now you boast in your arrogance. All such boasting is evil. Therefore, to him who knows to do good and does not do it, to him it is sin."* James 4:13-17.

So, without further ado, let us become familiar with the Spiritually Antiquated yet viably relevant *Rules of Royalty* we may have forgotten on this journey called life. Just so we are clear, before we move on, there are many *Rules of Royalty* that are only revealed based on our Spiritual Ranking. However, for this book, Spiritual Calculations, I have the Divine Authority to unveil the Foundational Principles of the Kingdom. However, if one desires to misuse these Spiritual Rules of Royalty selfishly, the veil would remain.

Royalty Rule One

The *Rules of Royalty* state that God requires Divine Order. If we cannot follow His instructions or hear His Voice, if we are Spiritually Blind, or if we have loose lips, we may view the Kingdom, but we will not enter. The *Spiritual Calculations* from the Heavenly of Heavens began in the Book of Genesis, setting the tone for Divine Order, then ending with the Book of Revelation, extending an Invitation to Servants who obeyed their Covenantal Responsibilities of the Kingdom. At the same time, it also rejects those who choose to become inhabitants or mere merchants.

How can I say such a thing about who is going to be accepted or rejected in the Kingdom? I am not pointing the finger; I am only unveiling the information and understanding needed for such a time as this. So, let us align this with scripture, *"And the <u>merchants</u> of the earth will weep and mourn over her, for no one buys their merchandise anymore."* Revelation 18:11. *"Then one of the seven angels who had the seven bowls came and talked with me, saying to me, Come, I will show you the judgment of the great harlot who sits on many waters, with whom the kings of the earth committed fornication, and the <u>inhabitants</u> of the earth were made drunk with the wine of her fornication."* Revelation 17:1-2. What is the meaning of this? It refers to our present-day worldliness and unrestrained lust contaminating our Mind, Body, and Soul, causing our Spirit to remain dormant.

With respect to all associations, this is one of the contributing factors to why people are not buying us or the charactorial facades we are offering. Due to this form of known or unknown rejection, we have to manipulate, bully, and whitewash the system, tainting our motives as we become a people-pleaser or a seemingly Holy Ghost-Filled individual without fire or staying power. How do we make this make sense? We play church without becoming the Temple of God or even knowing that the Kingdom of Heaven really exists.

When we play pretend, using our own rules to get into the Kingdom, God will sit us down in some way, shape, or form to get our attention. In this process, if we develop a deaf ear to Him, we cannot lay the blame elsewhere.

The Divine Relational Factors are predicated on our developing and maintaining a relationship with God, first and foremost. Secondly, once our Godly relationship is established and our Spirit is Awakened, we have the authority to use the bonding yet Fatherly relationship to build ourselves from the inside out. How is this possible? It is done with the proper use of the Fruits of the Spirit and Christlike Character. Thirdly, once accomplished, we must share our Servanthood with others through what we call our people skills.

As it relates to the *Rules of Royalty*, if this relational aspect of Divine Order does not occur, our Spiritual Rankings will not happen, and we are left to play pretend. What does this mean? There are Levels to Spirituality, and if we cannot get the first Rule of Order correct, we will fumble on the second, and so on. Plus, our fruits will give us away to those of a higher Spiritual Ranking; therefore, the only person we are really fooling is ourselves. Why are we fooling ourselves? It is due to our lack of understanding and respect for all things Spiritual.

Clearly, God loves us all, and He will meet us where we are, but when it comes down to the Secrets of the Kingdom, Divine Order must occur. If not, we become like the Pharisees and Sadducees, focused on judging and dragging others through the dirt for the same things we are secretly or openly guilty of under a different label. What does the Bible say about this? It says, *"Do not speak evil of one another, brethren. He who speaks evil of a brother and judges his brother, speaks evil of the law and judges the law. But if you judge the law, you are not a doer of the law but a judge. There is one Lawgiver, who is able to save and to destroy. Who are you to judge another?"* James 4:11-12.

The bottom line is that the goal of Divine Order is to relate, build, help, nurture, and understand. Without understanding the Nature of God, our nature, and the nature of another, we will find ourselves on a slippery slope, not having a clue about the Cycle of Life, forfeiting our rights to the *Spiritual Calculations* of the Kingdom. Yet, all is not lost; let us go deeper into the *Rules of Royalty*.

Royalty Rule Two

The *Rules of Royalty* state that God requires us to keep His Commands with clean hands and a pure, repenting heart. In the Kingdom, we are not big on showboating, period. We focus on the intents of the heart. Our motives supersede what we are doing, regardless of whether it is for ourselves, others, or the Kingdom. If our hearts are not right, *As It Pleases God*, it also indicates that our thoughts are not right as well, and vice versa.

More importantly, if repenting is not taking place or if our conscience is not convicting us when we err, it means the Holy Spirit is not setting the tonality of our lives; we are. The Kingdom cannot use self-led individuals. Why are self-led Believers overlooked? They are not overlooked per se; they are benched because we will get another Saul-like Spirit or a wolf in sheep's clothing, trying to kill or cripple those who are truly after God's own heart. For this reason, one must become Spirit-Led to avoid becoming misled, misleading, or harsh to the innocent and guilty alike. When we are Spirit-Led, we will notice that we will become gentle in our approach to God, ourselves, and others. Really? Yes, really. Philippians 4:5 says it all: *"Let your gentleness be known to all men. The Lord is at hand."*

Royalty Rule Three

The *Rules of Royalty* state that God requires Oneness from us, getting rid of our selfish ambitions while maximizing our relational people skills. Communication bridges the gap in any relationship. The moment we stop communicating, the bond of a relationship breaks by default. *"Therefore if there is any consolation in Christ, if any comfort of love, if any fellowship of the Spirit, if any affection and mercy, fulfill my joy by being like-minded, having the same love, being of one accord, of one mind. Let nothing be done through selfish ambition or conceit, but in lowliness of mind let each esteem others better than himself."* Philippians 2:1-3. How do we become One with God? Here is a list, but not limited to such:

- ☐ We must accept God as our Source and Creator of all things.

- ☐ We must call forth and awaken our Spirit, becoming willing to do the Will of God with truth and conviction.

- ☐ We must accept becoming One with the Holy Trinity (The Father, Son, and Holy Spirit).

☐ We must confess weaknesses, corruption, yokes, soul ties, or sins through praying, forgiving, and repenting, and for some things, fasting is needed.

☐ We must avail ourselves to the Spiritual Cleansing or Baptism, regrafting the old with the Newness of the Kingdom, getting rid of any idolatrous relationships or connections, as well as rotten morals, fruits, and biases.

☐ We must become open to the Spiritual Classroom or Training needed to prepare us to become Kingdom Material.

☐ We must familiarize ourselves with the Word and Voice of God, filtering out the negative, unproductive inner or outer chatter.

☐ We must begin to actively use the Fruits of the Spirit in our daily lives to erect the Tree of Life from within.

☐ We must avail ourselves to becoming Christlike in our charactorial behaviors, living by example.

☐ We must surrender to the use of our Gifts, Callings, and Talents as God ordains, becoming better every day while documenting our progress.

☐ We must become desensitized to the worldly means of accomplishing the Will of God.

☐ Once we are Spiritually Anointed, Trained, and Commissioned in Earthen Vessels, *As It Pleases God*, we must become willing to do what needs to be done for the Kingdom of Heaven. And then, replenishing from God's reservoir daily for instructions, assignments, lessons, or whatever.

In all honesty, this is not an overnight process; it will take time. So, do not rush the process. The Classroom of Life is unrelentingly brutal, especially if there is any form of disobedience involved.

According to the *Spiritual Calculations* of the Heavenly of Heavens, if we are ill-prepared not to use the Spiritual Tools of the Kingdom, we will become easily swept away through our own devices of misunderstanding. What does this mean? We cannot contend on a Spiritual Level when we have not been adequately trained to do so, even if we feel well-equipped.

The *Rules of Royalty* of the Kingdom are not just about knowing the Bible; it is about applying it in our daily lives. It is also about knowing why we are doing what we do and the benefits, consequences, and implications.

More importantly, the *'Kingdom Not To Do'* is equally vital to earning our Kingdom Credentials. As a rule, God will Spiritually Train us in stages, commissioning us to the next level when we are ready or adequately seasoned.

Now, depending upon what level we are on, it determines our level of responsibility or chastening regarding the use or misuse of the Spiritual Training, Tools, or Lessons given. So, we should not rush this process. Misused Spiritual Lessons, Secrets, or Power bring about generational curses, similar to Saul's experience in 1 Samuel.

Royalty Rule Four

The *Rules of Royalty* state that God wants a good report from us, period. What is a good report? Having something good to say in our moments of trials, tribulations, and testing.

How can we encourage ourselves when we are going through? Here is a scripture I use as a form of encouragement: "*My brethren, count it all joy when you fall into various trials, knowing that the testing of your faith produces patience. But let patience have its perfect work, that you may be perfect and complete, lacking nothing.*" James 1:2-4.

If we question ourselves regarding this scripture, it can and will change our mindsets. How do we go about doing so? Here is how

I would use it from a positive perspective when journaling my responses, but not limited to such questions:

- Why am I in this situation, circumstance, event, or Spiritual Classroom?
- What am I counting as joyful? Why is it joyful?
- How can I create a win-win or flip the script?
- What can I learn from this testing to be a Blessing?
- How can I proactively put my faith into action?
- How will my faith and patience benefit the Kingdom?
- What Fruits of the Spirit can I use to become better or fight off the sting of bitterness?
- Where can I create an opportunity with this lesson?
- How will this enhance my walk with God?
- Am I exhibiting Christlike Character?
- What type of wisdom can I glean to complete my good report for my Testament, Testimony, or the Kingdom?

When answering these questions or making up our own, we must stay on the positive side of the spectrum. Negativity, selfishness, vindictiveness, and doubt have no place in the Kingdom. It makes us wishy-washy and inconsistent. Really? Yes, really! But before we move on, let us align this with scripture, "*If any of you lacks wisdom, let him ask of God, who gives to all liberally and without reproach, and it will be given to him. But let him ask in faith, with no doubting, for he who doubts is like a wave of the sea driven and tossed by the wind. For let not that man suppose that he will receive anything from the Lord; he is a double-minded man, unstable in all his ways.*" James 1:5-8.

By far, this concept is similar to having a good report like Joshua and Caleb, as opposed to a negative report like the spies in Numbers 13. The Kingdom does not need a negative person who thrives on zapping our hope from within. Regardless of how life seems, we are required to have a Positive Mental Mindset, creating a win-win out of everything. How is this possible to do in a negative situation? It is done by repeating or keeping in mind Philippians 4:13, "*I can do all things through Christ who strengthens me.*"

What is the purpose of going through the testing phase only to have a good report? It is not just about a good report; it is positioning ourselves in the Kingdom to gain our Credentials or our Crown. I know this sounds like a fairytale, especially when dealing with real-life issues, right? Well, let us take it to scripture, which says, "*Blessed is the man who endures temptation; for when he has been approved, he will receive the Crown of Life which the Lord has promised to those who love Him.*" James 1:12.

When it is all said and done, the key is to endure, keeping One mind. How is this possible? We must come into an Oneness with the Holy Trinity. Developing this personal relationship helps us reel our thoughts in without going all the way to the left or overboard. Is it this simple? It depends upon our Spiritual Level or Eliteness, but James 4:8 advises, "*Therefore submit to God. Resist the devil and he will flee from you. Draw near to God and He will draw near to you. Cleanse your hands, you sinners; and purify your hearts, you double-minded.*" James 4:7-8.

Royalty Rule Five

The *Rules of Royalty* state that God wants us to proactively care about, respect, and look out for each other. We are our brother's keeper. How is this possible when we are barely responsible for our own lives? God does not require us to fix lives; He wants us to do our part, keeping others' best interests at heart as He BLESSES us to become a BLESSING. Is this Biblical? Let us take it to scripture, "*Let each of you look out not only for his own interests, but also for the interests of others. Let this mind be in you which was also in Christ Jesus.*" Philippians 2:4-5.

When proactively using the Fruits of the Spirit and Christlike Character, we will be surprised by how it brings life to another. Trust me, this goes further than we could ever imagine. It keeps our hands Blessed to receive when the tables turn in our favor or in our moment of need, especially when it comes down to things money cannot buy.

Royalty Rule Six
The *Rules of Royalty* state that God wants us to utilize the Fruits of the Spirit (Love, Joy, Peace, Patience, Kindness, Goodness, Faithfulness, Gentleness, and Self-Control) to help us govern ourselves accordingly. What is more, as it relates to the *Spiritual Calculations* of the Heavenly of Heavens, the Fruits of the Spirit create an open door to exhibiting Christlike Character, especially if we are not accustomed to doing so. In addition, it also puts us on the Leading Edge of Spirituality at its best, polishing up our work ethics for the Kingdom.

Why do we need to work for the Kingdom? We have free will to put in the work wherever and for whomever, but we must also keep in mind what the scripture advises. *"Do not seal the words of the prophecy of this book, for the time is at hand. He who is unjust, let him be unjust still; he who is filthy, let him be filthy still; he who is righteous, let him be righteous still; he who is holy, let him be holy still. And behold, I am coming quickly, and My reward is with Me, to give to every one according to his work. I am the Alpha and the Omega, the Beginning and the End, the First and the Last. Blessed are those who do His commandments, that they may have the right to the Tree of Life, and may enter through the gates into the city."* Revelation 22:10-14.

Now, the question is, 'What is on the Tree of Life?' The Tree of Life possesses the Fruits of the Spirit. As Spiritual Beings having a human experience in Earthen Vessels, without possessing the personal, private, professional, or communal fruits, *As It Pleases God*, we have limited access to Divine Wisdom, Treasures, Secrets, Power, and our Divine Blueprint. Even if we pretend to have Divine Access to them, our words, thoughts, beliefs, actions, and reactions will rat us out every single time. Really? Yes, really!

In the Kingdom of God, the Fruit of Divine Wisdom, the Fruit of Divine Treasures, the Fruit of Divine Secrets, the Fruit of Divine Power, the Fruit of Divine Purpose, the Fruit of Divine Understanding, and the Fruit of Divine Downloads all mean something in the Eye of God. How so? The Holy Spirit is the Divine Gateway to them all, and it is the Blood of Jesus that Divinely

Covers us in this Spiritual Realm. Therefore, it requires us to become rooted with positive character traits or behave Christlike to gain Spiritual Access, *As It Pleases God*.

Our roots run deep from within, and if they are corrupt without repentance or correction, we have bigger issues than what meets the eye. Plus, when gaining Divine Access without Spiritual Permission or with blatant corruption, it will cause us more harm psychologically than good. When dealing with Kingdom Royalty from the Heavenly of Heavens, we cannot play around with inner corruption because the conscience will kick our butts, especially behind closed doors when we proclaim Holiness, dabbling in unholiness.

What if we are really Holy and are having internal issues as Believers? We must check our Spiritual Fruits first. Here are a few questions to pinpoint the reason for the warring within the psyche, but not limited to such:

- ☐ Are we loving? Are we exhibiting love to others? Do we love ourselves?
- ☐ Are we joyful? Do we bring joy to the lives of others?
- ☐ Are we peaceful? Are we at peace with ourselves or others?
- ☐ Are we patient? Are we patient with ourselves or others?
- ☐ Are we kind? Are we kind to ourselves and others?
- ☐ Are we good people? Are we good to ourselves and others?
- ☐ Are we faithful? Are we faithful to ourselves and others?
- ☐ Are we gentle? Are we gentle with ourselves and others?
- ☐ Do we exhibit self-control? Can we control ourselves, our words, thoughts, beliefs, and desires?

Once done, the second step is to check our level of forgiveness. We would be surprised by how unforgiveness has a way of hiding itself under layers of something else with a hidden trigger. How is this humanly possible, especially when having great people skills? Regardless of whether we have good people skills or not, if the psyche is acting up, within the traits listed above lies a seed or root of something that the conscience is alerting us about. As the narrative unfolds, whether good, bad, or indifferent, it is our responsibility to deal with them accordingly. If not, then we cannot lay the blame elsewhere because the conscience did what it was designed to do...Warn us!

Royalty Rule Seven

The *Rules of Royalty* state that God wants us to put away the desire to complain, bicker, fuss, or fight. We must also squash jealousy, envy, pride, arrogance, anger, hatefulness, and coveting to the core.

Why should we use the *'Cease and Desist Clause'* from within? According to the *Spiritual Calculations* of the Heavenly of Heavens, we must become proactive in uprooting or regrafting any seeds of contention. Is this Biblical? Of course, *"The beginning of strife is like releasing water; therefore stop contention before a quarrel starts. He who justifies the wicked, and he who condemns the just, both of them alike are an abomination to the LORD."* Proverbs 17:14-15. Whether we feel like the bigger or smaller person, accountability is a must.

God wants us to take a second look at the small Blessings while becoming grateful for all things. Ungratefulness and impatience will get us barred from the Kingdom due to our lack of maneuverability and resourcefulness to extract the good out of a seemingly bad situation or the good out of an excellent opportunity. How is this possible if we are devout Believers? According to scripture: *"Therefore be patient, brethren, until the coming of the Lord. See how the farmer waits for the precious fruit of the earth, waiting patiently for it until it receives the early and latter rain. You also be patient. Establish your hearts, for the coming of the Lord is at hand. Do not grumble against one another, brethren, lest you be condemned. Behold, the Judge is standing at the door! My brethren, take the prophets, who spoke in the name of the Lord, as an example of suffering and patience. Indeed we count them blessed who endure. You have heard of the perseverance of Job and seen the end intended by the Lord—that the Lord is very compassionate and merciful."* James 5:7-11.

To acquire Kingdom Privileges, we cannot become Spiritually Blind, Deaf, or Mute to how Spiritual Laws work, such as Seedtime and Harvest, the Law of Reciprocity, the Law of Gravity, and the list goes on. What does this have to do with the Kingdom? We must become open to Opportunity, period.

Wherever there is a lack, there is also a Spiritual Opportunity; we simply need to ask, seek, knock, and find, leaving no stone unturned. Here is the scripture, *"But I rejoiced in the Lord greatly that now at last your care for me has flourished again; though you surely did care, but you lacked opportunity. Not that I speak in regard to need, for I have learned in whatever state I am, to be content: I know how to be abased, and I know how to abound. Everywhere and in all things I have learned both to be full and to be hungry, both to abound and to suffer need."* Philippians 4:10-12.

The goal is to keep a Positive Mindset, looking for the good, positive, and creative opportunities hidden in plain sight. Complaining, bickering, fussing, and fighting are all distractions that break our focus, causing Spiritual Blindness, Deafness, Muteness, or Paralysis.

So, whenever there is an obstacle, we must behave, think, and perform the opposite of an ordinary provocation. *"A fool vents all his feelings, but a wise man holds them back."* Proverbs 29:11. We do not have to give a person a piece of our minds, especially when we have the opportunity to learn, grow, and sow back into the Kingdom. Listed below are a few examples, but not limited to such:

- ☐ When something terrible happens, search for the opportunity or the win-win to become better as opposed to bitter. *"He who has an ear, let him hear what the Spirit says to the churches. To him who overcomes I will give to eat from the Tree of Life, which is in the midst of the Paradise of God."* Revelations 2:7.

- ☐ If the desire to complain presents itself, look for the opportunity to respond with compliments. *"Pleasant words are like a honeycomb, sweetness to the soul and health to the bones."* Proverbs 16:24.

- ☐ The moment an urge to fight piques a desire from within, look for the opportunity to respond peacefully without becoming emotional or combative. "*A soft answer turns away wrath, but a harsh word stirs up anger.*" Proverbs 15:1.

☐ When someone speaks nasty, disrespectful, or unruly to us, look for the opportunity to respond kindly without provocation. "*The tongue of the wise uses knowledge rightly, but the mouth of fools pours forth foolishness.*" Proverbs 15:2.

☐ When we are tempted to do wrong, look for the opportunity to do the right thing or the high road. "*The eyes of the LORD are in every place, beholding evil and the good.*" Proverbs 15:3.

☐ When we feel as if we want to fuss, we look for the opportunity to ask fact-finding, level-headed questions, getting the mental wheels for both parties turning in the right direction of righteousness. "*A wholesome tongue is a Tree of Life, but perverseness in it breaks the Spirit.*" Proverbs 15:4.

☐ When we feel the need to break someone down to the core, we look for the opportunity to build them up Mentally, Physically, Emotionally, and Spiritually. "*There is one who speaks like a piercing of a sword, but the tongue of the wise promotes health.*" Proverbs 12:18.

☐ When we are tempted to tell a lie or become a talebearer, look for the opportunity to exhibit wholesomeness or outright plead the 5th. "*Better is a dry morsel with quietness, than a house full of feasting with strife.*" Proverbs 17:1.

☐ When we are tempted to pay someone back, look for the opportunity to Bless them instead. "*Her ways are ways of pleasantness, and all her paths are peace. She is a Tree of Life to those who take hold of her, and happy are all who retain her.*" Proverbs 3:17-18.

- ☐ When we have a desire to become rebellious, we must look for the opportunity and the benefits associated with obedience. *"The ear that hears the rebukes of life will abide among the wise. He who disdains instruction despises his own soul, but he who heeds rebuke gets understanding. The fear of the LORD is the instruction of wisdom, and before honor is humility."* Proverbs 15:31-33.

- ☐ When we begin to develop ulterior motives to violate the will of another, we look for an opportunity to become an asset and not a liability. *"Every way of a man is right in his own eyes, but the LORD weighs the hearts. To do righteousness and justice is more acceptable to the LORD than sacrifice."* Proverbs 21:2-3.

- ☐ When we feel as if we need to pick on, laugh at, or bully others, look for the opportunity to become a Blessing. We do not know what God is doing in that person's life, nor do we know who they are ordained to become. More importantly, according to scripture: *"He who mocks the poor reproaches his Maker; He who is glad at calamity will not go unpunished."* Proverbs 17:5.

Why do we need to reverse the negative to create a win-win situation? If we indulge in negativity, we bring it back to ourselves. Is this Biblical? It says, *"Whoever digs a pit will fall into it, and he who rolls a stone will have it roll back on him."* Proverbs 26:27. As a part of the Kingdom, we cannot ignore this one fact; therefore, if we look for the opportunity, win-win, or positive, we can develop a Kingdom Mentality with Spiritual Credentials to back it up.

Our Fruits of the Spirit and Christlike Character will become evident in our basic Method of Operation without having to say one word or convince anyone—it is the Natural Voila of the Kingdom. How? The use of the Fruits of the Spirit and Christlike Character avails us of unseen opportunity before it manifests into reality. For this reason, we must pay them forward to create a pathway of least resistance.

Believe it or not, the Book of Proverbs is loaded with Kingdom Ethics, giving us the benefits and repercussions of good and evil, positive and negative, as well as right and wrong. By far, this is how I learned, and I know beyond a shadow of a doubt it will open the eyes of those who have a willingness to embrace the Tree of Life and not just see it from afar. What will this do for us? It will give us the *'Iron Sharpens Iron Mentality'* that Proverbs 27:17 speaks of.

Royalty Rule Eight
The *Rules of Royalty* state that God wants us to become hopefully faithful. To become faithful, we must master the ability to use our faith, making it work on our behalf. Our faith is not something we put on the shelf for a later date; our faith is proactively in the now. What does this mean? Let us align this with scripture, *"For as the body without the spirit is dead, so faith without works is dead also."* James 2:26.

How can we work our faith according to Kingdom Standards? The moment we make a conscious decision to awaken our faith through the Holy Spirit, it will respond with interchangeable hope. Frankly, the more we use them together, the stronger they become while symbolically manifesting into a form of Spiritual Glue for other areas of our lives.

To embrace this form of Spiritual Glue's totality, we must put our faith in the Source of it. We cannot discount a Greater Hope of Spiritual Knowing from within. When we know the Holy Trinity has our back, we will walk in the Will of God without any form of reservation. What does this mean? According to the *Spiritual Calculations* of the Heavenly of Heavens, this form of Spiritual Glue is Marked!

The Holy Trinity is residing and presiding where trust in this Spiritual Glue exists. Just so we are clear, the illusion of hope or faith will also reside in our pompousness or selfishness as well. The difference is that Spiritual Glue has real manifesting power, and the illusion does not unless we tread upon the dark side for superficial power, resulting in severe consequences later on. How do we know which one we are operating under? It is often revealed in a crisis or when placed under pressure. For this reason, God will place us in a Spiritual Classroom, break us, and then test us before Commissioning.

Why would God take us through the motions? Frankly, for this question, let us take it to scripture, *"For by Him all things were created that are in heaven and that are on earth, visible and invisible, whether thrones or dominions or principalities or powers. All things were created through Him and for Him."* Colossians 1:16. What does this mean? Everything belongs to God. He has His reasoning for doing what He does whenever He does it. Our job is to trust the Will of God and His Divine Timing without becoming unglued at the seams.

Royalty Rule Nine

The *Rules of Royalty* state that God wants us to gain Spiritual Insight of understanding, knowledge, and wisdom from a Kingdom Perspective. He wants us to have Spiritual Access to the Treasures of Heaven. Here is the scripture, *"For I want you to know what a great conflict I have for you and those in Laodicea, and for as many as have not seen my face in the flesh, that their hearts may be encouraged, being knit together in love, and attaining to all riches of the full assurance of understanding, to the knowledge of the mystery of God, both of the Father and of Christ, in whom are hidden all the treasures of wisdom and knowledge."* Colossians 2:1-3.

In the *Spiritual Calculations* of our transformational process, we are required to do our part. We do not have to be rocket scientists; we only need to become Servants to the Kingdom, obeying the Covenant. *"For our Citizenship is in Heaven, from which we also eagerly wait for the Savior, the Lord Jesus Christ, who will transform our lowly body that it may be conformed to His glorious body, according to the working by which He is able even to subdue all things to Himself."* Philippians 3:20-21.

What is the takeaway when we comply with the *Rules of Royalty*? First and foremost, God can and will use anyone because He is no respecter of persons. Secondly, when in our purifying and testing phase, if we live by this scripture, *"He knows the way that I take; when*

He has tested me, I shall come forth as pure gold." Job 23:10. Coming forth as pure gold, *As It Pleases God,* will change the trajectory of our lives by default. We are not rebelling against the Will of God; instead, we are willfully availing ourselves to the process. Thirdly, in the induction phase of the Kingdom, we are classified in a relational capacity as a *'Friend of the World'* or the *'Enemy of God.'*

Before becoming Spiritually Married into the Kingdom, we will be thoroughly tested to see if we will obey the *Rules of Royalty* or become disobedient. What is the purpose of classification in the Kingdom? Let us take it to scripture, which says, *"Adulterers and adulteresses! Do you not know that friendship with the world is enmity with God? Whoever therefore wants to be a friend of the world makes himself an enemy of God. Or do you think that the Scripture says in vain, 'The Spirit who dwells in us yearns jealously?' But He gives more grace. Therefore He says: 'God resists the proud, but gives grace to the humble.' Therefore submit to God. Resist the devil and he will flee from you."* James 4:4-7.

The *Royalty of our Kingdom* is a non-violation zone, and if we want all God has to offer, here is our motivation: *"And the Spirit and the bride say, 'Come!' And let him who hears say, 'Come!' And let him who thirsts come. Whoever desires, let him take the water of life freely."* Revelation 22:17. Here is what we need to know about the Kingdom of Heaven's *Spiritual Calculations:*

- ☐ We are Blessed to be a Blessing.
- ☐ We will fall as a Blessing or fall into a Blessing for purification.
- ☐ We will become restored because of our Covenantal Birthrights or Blessings.

Knowing these three factors alters our perception from worldly to Spiritual. Now, let us take it to scripture, *"Then he said to me, Write: 'Blessed are those who are called to the marriage supper of the Lamb!' And he said to me, these are the true sayings of God."* Revelation 19:9. More importantly, willfully applying the *Rules of Royalty* in our lives without forfeiting them in the processing phase will cause God to create a Divinely Ordained lifestyle for us. How? It is done by making this one scripture factual and applicable: *"Every place that the sole of your foot will tread upon I have given you, as I said to Moses."* Joshua 1:3.

What about the places we do not set the soles of our feet on? It is not ours! What belongs to us will come, period. However, we must know this beyond a shadow of a doubt. If not, the enemy will sow tares among our wheat. But if we stand steadfast to the *Rules of Royalty*, here is the decree: *"No man shall be able to stand before you all the days of your life; as I was with Moses, so I will be with you. I will not leave you nor forsake you."* Joshua 1:5.

Royalty Rule Ten
The *Rules of Royalty* state that God wants us to become rooted and grounded in the Word of God to avoid being led astray, deceived, or playing the blaming game. Why is this so important? It is so easy to blame God when we make a mess to avoid taking responsibility or when we are playing in the shadows without seeking the Light. Here is what God has to say about this matter: *"Let no one say when he is tempted, I am tempted by God; for God cannot be tempted by evil, nor does He Himself tempt anyone. But each one is tempted when he is drawn away by his own desires and enticed. Then, when desire has conceived, it gives birth to sin; and sin, when it is full-grown, brings forth death. Do not be deceived, my beloved brethren. Every good gift and every perfect gift is from above, and comes down from the Father of Lights, with whom there is no variation or shadow of turning."* James 1:13-17.

We have three types of categories we must contend with: the Lust of the Flesh, the Lust of the Eyes, and the Pride of Life. Everything we do, say, and become will fall under one of those three categories if we do not become rooted and grounded in the Word of God according to the Kingdom of Heaven. What can we do to help ourselves? Let us take it to scripture: *"So then, my beloved brethren, let every man be swift to hear, slow to speak, slow to wrath; for the wrath of man does not produce the righteousness of God. Therefore lay aside all* filthiness and overflow of wickedness, and receive with meekness the implanted word, which is able to save your souls. But be doers of the word, and not hearers only, deceiving yourselves." James 1:19-22.

When it comes down to Kingdom Principles and Secrets, "It is the glory of God to conceal a matter, but the Glory of Kings is to search out a matter." Proverbs 25:2. Why do we need to search? It gives us staying power in the Kingdom. If it does not cost us anything, we will feel as if we can walk in and out at our leisure without putting in the work or becoming accountable. By knowing the Word for ourselves, it helps us to understand a few things, but not limited to such:

- ☐ When deception is at our back door, and when it is not.
- ☐ When God is speaking and when He is not.
- ☐ When the Holy Spirit is nudging us and when He is not.
- ☐ When our Inside Voice is speaking and when it is not.
- ☐ When our conscience is being violated, and when it is not.
- ☐ When we are in alignment and when we are out of order.
- ☐ When to hold, when to fold, and when to walk away.
- ☐ When to move forward and when to fall back.
- ☐ When to engage and when to disengage.
- ☐ When to stand up and when to stand down.
- ☐ When to speak and when to hold our tongue or plead the 5th.
- ☐ When to pay attention, and when to block something or someone out, Mentally, Physically, Emotionally, or Spiritually, to safeguard ourselves.

In addition, it assists us in living life the way God intended, and not on our own terms, living clueless, ungoverned, reckless, and worldly. Here is what scripture has to say, "Now this I say lest anyone should deceive you with persuasive words. For though I am absent in the flesh, yet I am with you in spirit, rejoicing to see your good order and the steadfastness of your faith in Christ. As you therefore have received Christ Jesus the Lord, so *walk in Him, rooted and built up in Him and established in the faith, as you have been taught, abounding in it with thanksgiving. Beware lest anyone cheat you through philosophy and empty deceit, according to the tradition of men, according to the basic principles of the world, and not according to Christ."* Colossians 2:4-8.

Royalty Rule Eleven

The *Rules of Royalty* state that God wants us to become a Kingdom Steward. Our Stewardship is not a role that should be taken for granted. Working for the Kingdom is an honor and privilege, not a burden. If God is a burden, one must rethink their role. With all due respect, if it were not for the Kingdom of Heaven, we would not exist.

For example, I am required to bring forth the unadulterated truth from the Heavenly of Heavens; therefore, when it comes down to the Kingdom, it is a responsibility. Furthermore, if we are feeling some form of burden, then there is some form of irresponsibility or error in the camp. We cannot expect to receive the Secrets of the Kingdom when our hearts are burdened with chains. Why not? We will become irresponsible or reckless due to the condition of our hearts.

What can we do to make a change? We must reconcile ourselves back into the Kingdom of Heaven as Paul did in Colossians 1:19-23. *"For it pleased the Father that in Him all the fullness should dwell, and by Him to reconcile all things to Himself, by Him, whether things on earth or things in heaven, having made peace through the blood of His cross. And you, who once were alienated and enemies in your mind by wicked works, yet now He has reconciled in the body of His flesh through death, to present you holy, and blameless, and above reproach in His sight—if indeed you continue in the faith, grounded and steadfast, and are not moved away from the hope of the gospel which you heard, which was preached to every creature under heaven, of which I, Paul, became a minister."*

Royalty Rule Twelve

The *Rules of Royalty* state that God wants us to properly govern ourselves with a Heavenly Mindset. Worldly disobedience becomes kryptonite, keeping us bound Mentally, Physically, Emotionally, and Spiritually. Now, if this is what we desire, then so be it.

However, for the Kingdom, we are called to a higher standard. If we fall short for whatever reason or however, we must become ever so repenting with the work-in-progress mentality of betterment, not bitterness. Why is this so important? When we are representing the Kingdom, we cannot indulge in any and everything or with everyone. Even if someone attempts to hang us out to dry regarding a mistake or our past, our Heavenly Mindset will come in to assist us if we learn how to use it accordingly.

When or if we indulge, we must make a conscious attempt to set ourselves back on the right course of righteousness, embracing the Spiritual Newness that is available to us every single day through prayer, repentance, and sometimes fasting. Here is the decree: "*Therefore put to death your members which are on the earth: fornication, uncleanness, passion, evil desire, and covetousness, which is idolatry. Because of these things the wrath of God is coming upon the sons of disobedience, in which you yourselves once walked when you lived in them. But now you yourselves are to put off all these: anger, wrath, malice, blasphemy, filthy language out of your mouth. Do not lie to one another, since you have put off the old man with his deeds, and have put on the new man who is renewed in knowledge according to the image of Him who created him, where there is neither Greek nor Jew, circumcised nor uncircumcised, barbarian, Scythian, slave nor free, but Christ is all and in all.*" Colossians 3:5-11.

Just so we are clear regarding a Heavenly Mindset, no one is absolutely perfect or without flaws, even if they pretend to be such. According to the *Spiritual Calculations* and the *Rules of Royalty*, we must work on ourselves daily, crucifying our flesh and renewing our Mind, Body, Soul, and Spirit while maximizing our ability to forgive and exhibit mercy. We will never know when we may need it for ourselves or our loved ones. For this reason, we should always pay this *Rule of Royalty* forward because it gives us Spiritual Leverage in the Kingdom.

What if we feel like fools to forgive and have mercy? Spiritually, we only behave foolishly when we do not forgive, exhibit mercy, and show compassion. Forgiveness, mercy, or compassion is not used for their sake; it is for ours.

Unforgiveness, malice, anger, hatefulness, debauchery, cruelness, or coveting nullify our Kingdom Privileges and inner healing, weighing down the human psyche by default. Most often, we think this makes us strong, when in all actuality, it makes us secretly weak, gullible, and insecure, giving way or leaving an open door for the enemy to sift us through the thoughts and opinions of others.

Having hurt feelings or a bruised ego does not equate to becoming disqualified in the Kingdom. How is this possible when we were offended? Being offended does not mean we should forget about the *Rules of Royalty* or our role in the situation. Why do we need to bear our share of responsibility? Listed below are a few reasons, but not limited to such:

- ☐ We did not incorporate the Holy Trinity (The Father, Son, and Holy Spirit) into the equation.
- ☐ We allowed our emotions to overrule our sense of good judgment.
- ☐ We engaged in uncorrected thoughts, entertaining the offense.
- ☐ We did not get a full understanding or ask fact-finding questions before making assumptions.
- ☐ We chose not to let go of our Mental, Physical, and Emotional hang-ups to embrace the Spiritual Freedom of having a Heavenly Mindset.
- ☐ We are avoiding the use of the Fruits of the Spirit.
- ☐ We are not exhibiting Christlike Character.
- ☐ We did not create a win-win, allowing the negative to overshadow the positive.
- ☐ We are ignoring or denying the truth about the situation, circumstance, or event.
- ☐ We simply want to prove a point to ourselves or someone to satiate a vendetta.

- ☐ We are engaged in some form of bullying, manipulation, or mind control, catering to our hidden motives, setting someone up, or violating the privacy of another by snooping.
- ☐ We are in denial of our role, wrongness, or contribution to whatever the issue is or with whomever.

We can go on for days with this list; however, a worldly mindset comprised of negativity creates an injustice on our behalf. It is best to clean up our act before having the nerve to point the finger, refuse to forgive, deny mercy, or ignore the compassion needed to become our best selves. Remember, everything we need is already! So, our capacity to develop a Heavenly Mindset is within our reach; we simply need to stretch ourselves to reach beyond our self-imposed limitations into unlimited possibilities regarding how we view and engage in worldly matters from God's Perspective.

Royalty Rule Thirteen

The *Rules of Royalty* state that God wants us to understand that His Chosen Elect must behave in a Christlike manner. We cannot behave like a hellion on wheels, portraying this behavior as if it is from the Kingdom. Nor can we behave like a hellion behind closed doors, slandering the ones we proclaim to love. While at the same time pretending to be Heaven Sent in the public eye.

Of course, we are all a work-in-progress, and we will all have our moments; however, the correction or repenting process must occur quickly. Rationalizing and justifying misbehaving without correction leaves an open door for the enemy to sift us into worldliness, stealing our Kingdom Access. How can we lose our access? Unjustified or uncorrected unruliness can cause our Spiritual Mantle to transfer to the next in line, or we can outright abort our Blessing.

Listen, in the Kingdom, God is expecting us to get our thoughts and emotions under control, period. Is this Biblical? Of course, it says, *"Therefore, as the elect of God, holy and beloved, put on tender mercies,* kindness, humility, meekness, longsuffering; bearing with one another, and forgiving one another, if anyone has a complaint against another; even as Christ forgave you, so you also must do. But above all these things put on love, which is the bond of perfection. And let the peace of God rule in your hearts, to which also you were called in one body; and be thankful. Let the word of Christ dwell in you richly in all wisdom, teaching and admonishing one another in psalms and hymns and spiritual songs, singing with grace in your hearts to the Lord. And whatever you do in word or deed, do all in the name of the Lord Jesus, giving thanks to God the Father through Him." Colossians 3:12-17.

Royalty Rule Fourteen

The *Rules of Royalty* state that God wants us to become fair and impartial. The Kingdom frowns upon unjust dealings and favorable bribes. *"A wicked man accepts a bribe behind the back to pervert the ways of justice."* Proverbs 17:23. So be very careful. Here is a decree most of us are unaware of: *"Whoever rewards evil for good, evil will not depart from his house."* Proverbs 17:13.

Why do we need to know about being fair and impartial? *"To show partiality is not good, because for a piece of bread a man will transgress."* Proverbs 28:21. When we do anything to get ahead, we must bring ourselves in for questioning. It leads to all types of issues from the inside out. *"A gift in secret pacifies anger, and a bribe behind the back, strong wrath. It is a joy for the just to do justice, but destruction will come to the workers of iniquity."* Proverbs 21:14-15.

Furthermore, if we want fairness, give it. Without a doubt, fairness and equal rights keep our hands Blessed. In the Kingdom, right is right, and wrong is wrong. Better yet, let us take this one to Colossians 4:1: *"Masters, give your bondservants what is just and fair, knowing that you also have a Master in Heaven."*

Regardless of who we are and why we are, we must understand from a Kingdom Mentality that *"The poor man and the oppressor have this in common: The LORD gives light to the eyes of both."* Proverbs 29:13. Therefore, we must stay on a learning curve because we all can learn a little something from everyone. How is it possible to learn from everyone? We need to begin with a few things, but not limited to such:

- ☐ We must take our blinders off to see what is in plain sight.
- ☐ We must unplug our ears to hear what is being verbalized audibly as well as inaudibly.
- ☐ We must set a guard over our mouths to articulate in a way to reach those we would not reach otherwise.

What is the purpose of knowing and applying these items? *"Those who forsake the law praise the wicked, but such as keep the law contends with them. Evil men do not understand justice, but those who seek the LORD understand all. Better is the poor who walks in his integrity than one perverse in his ways, though he be rich."* Proverbs 28:4-6.

Royalty Rule Fifteen
The *Rules of Royalty* state that God wants us to pray, give thanks, and peacefully speak the Word of God, bringing life to another by building them up without tearing them down. Our Heavenly Language is designed to ignite the Light from within, and if we are dimming or putting out the Light in ourselves or another, we have work to do. According to scripture: *"Continue earnestly in prayer, being vigilant in it with thanksgiving; meanwhile praying also for us, that God would open to us a door for the word, to speak the mystery of Christ, for which I am also in chains, that I may make it manifest, as I ought to speak. Walk in wisdom toward those who are outside, redeeming the time. Let your speech always be with grace, seasoned with salt, that you may know how you ought to answer each one."* Colossians 4:2-6.

Royalty Rule Sixteen
The *Rules of Royalty* state that God wants us to seek His approval, As It Pleases Him, and not the approval of men. We must become responsible for the spoken and unspoken Word of God without tampering with it to appease a worldly audience. Listen, we are the

Earthen Vessel God uses to accomplish His Divine Purpose. If we override what He wants with what we desire, in time, He will shut us down, if not Physically, but definitely Mentally, Emotionally, and Spiritually. Once again, this is why He puts us through vigorous tests, purifying our worldliness. *"But as we have been approved by God to be entrusted with the gospel, even so we speak, not as pleasing men, but God who tests our hearts. For neither at any time did we use flattering words, as you know, nor a cloak for covetousness—God is witness."* 1 Thessalonians 2:4-5.

Royalty Rule Seventeen

The *Rules of Royalty* state that God wants us to sow Mentally, Physically, Emotionally, and Spiritually into the Kingdom to reap the Hidden Secrets unknown to the untrained eye. The Kingdom Benefits are not given away to all who want them just because they want them. We have Spiritual Rules governing the output of the Heavenly Secrets or Treasures. Is this fair? Absolutely, we must put in the work to become Spiritually Unveiled.

Once we do, here is what Matthew 13:11 tells us: *"Because it has been given to you to know the mysteries of the Kingdom of Heaven, but to them it has not been given."* Why do they not receive the mysteries? *"For the hearts of this people have grown dull. Their ears are hard of hearing, and their eyes they have closed, lest they should see with their eyes and hear with their ears, lest they should understand with their hearts and turn, so that I should heal them. But blessed are your eyes for they see, and your ears for they hear; for assuredly, I say to you that many prophets and righteous men desired to see what you see, and did not see it, and to hear what you hear, and did not hear it."* Matthew 13:15-17.

If we allow the *Rules of Royalty* to permeate our lives, we will begin to see a big difference from the inside out. Kingdom Privileges have a covering, keys, and benefits that are not available to most; therefore, we do not have to engage in pompous behaviors to get attention or to appear Blessed—we just are. Here is what the scriptures say, *"Their descendants shall be known among the Gentiles, and their offspring among the people. All who see them shall acknowledge them, that they are the posterity whom the LORD has blessed. I will greatly rejoice in the*

LORD, My soul shall be joyful in my God; for He has clothed me with the garments of salvation, He has covered me with the robe of righteousness, as a bridegroom decks himself with ornaments, and as a bride adorns herself with her jewels. For as the earth brings forth its bud, as the garden causes the things that are sown in it to spring forth, So the Lord GOD will cause righteousness and praise to spring forth before all the nations."* Isaiah 61:9-12.

Royalty Rule Eighteen
The *Rules of Royalty* state that God wants us to guard our hearts, minds, and mouths to prevent us from defiling ourselves, becoming blind, or leading the blind into a ditch. We are accountable for defiling ourselves and others by what proceeds from our mouth's gateway, which ultimately stems from the heart. Really? Yes! *"Whoever guards his mouth and tongue keeps his soul from troubles."* Proverbs 21:23.

We must focus on inner sanctity instead of outer show or the lack thereof. Spiritually, this is why Matthew 15:13 says, *"Every Plant which My Heavenly Father has not planted will be uprooted."* What does this mean? The Kingdom of Heaven is within, and it is predicated on a regrafting process, expunging the old and ushering in the new.

Now, if we are full of evil debauchery without any form of Divine Revelation, it is a definite sign that we are not operating with Kingdom Credentials. Here is what we must know: *"Do you not yet understand that whatever enters the mouth goes into the stomach and is eliminated? But those things which proceed out of the mouth come from the heart, and they defile a man. For out of the heart proceed evil thoughts, murders, adulteries, fornications, thefts, false witness, and blasphemies. These are the things which defile a man, but to eat with unwashed hands does not defile a man."* Matthew 15:17-20.

God wants us to look from within, ensuring our hearts are right before judging someone for what they are putting in their stomach. The elements of the unseen are more powerful than the seen. How do we make this make sense? Let me counteract this question with another. Can we see our thoughts? No, we cannot; yet, they are very powerful, manifesting the unspoken into reality. Can we see our words? No, we cannot; yet, they are mighty, cutting wounds of trauma into the human psyche or healing it beyond our imagination. Can we see our emotions? No, we cannot; yet, they are compelling, putting us on a rollercoaster, instigating all types of illusions or untruths if not governed accordingly. Can we see our Mind, Soul, and Spirit? No, we cannot; yet, they are very powerful, working in unison to govern our Body in ways that will cause us to shake in our boots, suffer death from the inside out while still alive, or heal themselves in ways that are miraculous in nature.

Kingdom Salvation is not what we put in our mouths; it is what we ingest in our Minds and Souls that affect the Body, causing our Spirit to awaken or remain dormant. Just so we are clear, I am not saying to avoid eating healthy, abuse food, or not taking care of our Temples because we should. However, when it comes down to judging another man's rights in the Kingdom, it has nothing to do with us.

We are mere Vessels God uses to accomplish His Divine Purpose; therefore, if we take care of our part of the deal of not becoming defiled, He will take care of His.

Royalty Rule Nineteen
The *Rules of Royalty* state that God does not want us to become unequally yoked with those who thwart our entrance into the Kingdom of Heaven. Listed below are a few examples, but not limited to such:

- ☐ If someone or something is pulling us away from our Divine Purpose, Talent, or Calling, we are required to sever ties without being nasty, rude, mean, or demeaning.
- ☐ If they are instigating unrighteous dealings or behaviors, we must sever ties.
- ☐ If they are misleading us with false doctrine, negativity, or hate, we must sever ties.
- ☐ If they are initiating idol worship, we must sever ties.
- ☐ If they are blind, leading us into a ditch, we must sever ties.
- ☐ If they are intentionally sowing tares among our wheat to derail us, we must sever ties.

- ☐ If they are abusing, misusing, or traumatizing us, we must sever ties.
- ☐ If they are preying on our weaknesses, causing us to err, we must sever ties.
- ☐ If they are instigating mind-controlling tactics to cause us to violate Spiritual or Manmade Laws, we must sever ties.
- ☐ If they are always on the take with selfish behaviors, never contributing to anything or anyone, we must sever ties.
- ☐ If they are attempting to destroy us, Mentally, Physically, Emotionally, or Spiritually, we must sever ties.
- ☐ If they are zapping our Spiritual Power or Anointing, we must sever ties.

As the scripture states, *"Do not be unequally yoked together with unbelievers. For what fellowship has righteousness with lawlessness? And what communion has light with darkness?"* 2 Corinthians 6:14. Most often, we tend to use this particular scripture to judge other denominations serving the same God. However, in the Kingdom, we have the division of Light versus darkness and righteous versus unrighteous. Some people live better by nature, based upon the contents of their hearts, than those who proclaim to live by the Word of God. How can I say such a thing, right? I am only the Messenger, but I pay attention to the fruits of men, not their Religiosity. According to the *Rules of Royalty*, I am required to set the record straight. Proclaiming to be Godly or righteous does not make us so.

Our actions, behaviors, responses, demeanor, attitude, what we say, and motives determine our Heavenly Light or worldly darkness, as well as our righteousness or unrighteousness. What is the purpose of knowing this? According to scripture, *"The refining pot is for silver and the furnace for gold, but the LORD tests the hearts."* Proverbs 17:3. No one is exempt from this process, so we must consider our ways to gain Kingdom Access, *As It Pleases God*.

Royalty Rule Twenty

The *Rules of Royalty* state that God wants us to hear His Voice when He speaks. We must be able to hear the Voice of God for ourselves. The Kingdom frowns on Spiritual Codependency unless one is in a Spiritual Classroom, Fold, or Timeout. In essence, this is how God gives us instructions, warnings, advice, discernment, heightened instincts, and decrees, which are all vital when possessing Kingdom Credentials. It ensures we do not get caught off guard or with our hands in the cookie jar.

If we cannot hear the Voice of God, it will cause a secret decline out of the Kingdom; therefore, our Spiritual Senses must be exercised and on alert at all times. What is the purpose of doing so? The Treasures of the Kingdom are sought-after commodities by those who have access, those who want them, as well as those who cannot have them or who have been banned. For this reason, the ones who possess the Kingdom Credentials cannot showboat. It prevents them from becoming a target based on their weak spots, traumas, or handicaps.

Deception is always lurking to ensnare us, especially if we have Kingdom Credentials or if we are working to obtain them. Furthermore, suppose we do not receive Spiritual Forewarnings, Foresight, or Nudges, or we outright miss our cue. In this case, we can become side-swiped due to Spiritual Negligence, causing some form of division from the inside out. But, "*A prudent man foresees evil and hides himself, but the simple pass on and are punished.*" Proverbs 22:3. Why are we responsible if we do not recognize deception? Usually, this happens for two reasons:

- ☐ We ignore the signs.
- ☐ We willfully violated our conscience.

According to the *Spiritual Calculations* from the Heavenly of Heavens, we must place the Holy Spirit on high alert at all times, even when we are asleep. How is this possible? It is the Body that requires sleep or rest. All things unseen, such as our Minds, Souls, and Spirits, do not require sleep or rest. Yet, our Spirit will lie dormant when we allow our soulish nature to dominate or when our secretly or openly traumatized soul contaminates our minds with negativity, debauchery, or evil.

To connect with the Holy Spirit, we must consciously awaken our Spirit to become One, giving Him the authority to tame the Mind, Body, and Soul. Without Him, we are on our own, left to our own accord, doing what we do best in a bed of worldliness we will not understand without Spiritual Intervention. Frankly, I warn against this. *"Whoever has no rule over his own Spirit is like a city broken down, without walls."* Proverbs 25:28.

Even though we take this simple Biblical Principle for granted, let me share the power encapsulated in it. *"But You, O LORD, are a shield for me, my glory and the One who lifts up my head. I cried to the LORD with my voice, and He heard me from His holy hill. Selah. I lay down and slept; I awoke, for the LORD sustained me. I will not be afraid of ten thousands of people Who have set themselves against me all around. Arise, O LORD; Save me, O my God! For You have struck all my enemies on the cheekbone; You have broken the teeth of the ungodly. Salvation belongs to the LORD. Your blessing is upon Your people. Selah."* Psalm 3:3-8.

Based upon years of study, if we want to hear the real Voice of God or calm the negative chatter from within, we must awaken ourselves from our slumber, giving the Holy Spirit room to clean our inner Sanctuary, Temple, or House. Can we conduct our own spring cleaning from the inside out? Of course, we can; however, we will limit what we can do in our own strength.

Why do we need cleansing? In our own eyes, we cannot see ourselves unless there is an outside source reflecting an image on our behalf. Technically, this is similar to using a mirror to see a complete image of ourselves, whereas if we do it independently, the view is limited. For this reason, the scriptures tell us, *"Draw near to God and He will draw near to you. Cleanse your hands, you sinners; and purify your hearts, you double-minded. Lament and mourn and weep! Let your laughter be turned to mourning and your joy to gloom. Humble yourselves in the sight of the Lord, and He will lift you up."* James 4:8-10.

Royalty Rule Twenty-One

The *Rules of Royalty* state that God wants us to value having a good name, reputation, and accountability with Him, ourselves, and others. Why should we build value? Let me answer this question with another: *'What would it profit a man if he gained the whole world and lost his own soul? Or what will a man give in exchange for his soul?'* Matthew 16:26. For this reason, in the Kingdom, "*A good name is to be chosen rather than great riches, loving favor rather than silver and gold. The rich and the poor have this in common, The LORD is the maker of them all.*" Proverbs 22:1-2.

The *Mark of Royalty* has weight in the Kingdom. What is the *Mark*? It is FAVOR. Favorable Judgment in the Kingdom is a sought-after *Marking*, especially for those who have an Elite Status among the Heavenly of Heavens. Just so we are clear, earthly favor is not the same as Heavenly Favor, nor is it biased favoritism—it is equal rights Favor. Having Heavenly Favor or the Mark of Royalty is applicable in both places, whereas earthly favor is limited to the status and conditions of the individual offering it.

When we are Kingdom Marked, we are called to represent as a Servant, period! Whether it is a Servant Prophet, Teacher, Mentor, Shepherd, Mother, Father, Sister, Brother, or whatever, we are called to a higher standard to protect our Spiritual Marking. Is this Biblical? It says, "*In the middle of its street, and on either side of the river, was the tree of life, which bore twelve fruits, each tree yielding its fruit every month. The leaves of the tree were for the healing of the nations. And there shall be no more curse, but the Throne of God and of the Lamb shall be in it, and His <u>servants</u> shall serve Him. They shall see His face, and His name shall be on their foreheads. There shall be no night there: They need no lamp nor light of the sun, for the Lord God gives them light. And they shall reign forever and ever.*" Revelation 22:2-5.

Royalty Rule Twenty-Two

The *Rules of Royalty* state that God wants us to understand our Purpose, Mission, Calling, Talent, or Gifts from His point of view. If we do not know why we are here, we can become led astray by all types of distracting agendas, tossing us to and fro. What makes knowing this so important? By knowing who we are and why, we are better able to follow Divine Instructions, we are better able to focus on our pearls (the hidden Treasures) from within, we are more willing to become purified as fine gold, and we are open to transparency. Is this Biblical? Of course, *"The twelve gates were twelve pearls: each individual gate was of one pearl. And the street of the city was pure gold, like transparent glass."* Revelation 21:21.

Often enough, we paint an illusion of this scripture in our Mind's Eye of some sort of fairytale; however, according to the *Spiritual Calculations* of the Heavenly of Heavens, it is crystal clear that our Heaven on Earth experience is our reality, applying to our now. How is this possible? Let me break this down: Twelve equals instructions. Pearl equals the hidden treasures and tools associated with our Spiritual Reasoning (Why we are here). Pure equals filtering and training needed to possess the Promise or Birthright. And, transparency equals truthfulness and living by example. Once understood and applied, here is what happens according to Revelation 21:22-26: *"But I saw no temple in it, for the Lord God Almighty and the Lamb are its temple. The city had no need of the sun or of the moon to shine in it, for the glory of God illuminated it. The Lamb is its light. And the nations of those who are saved shall walk in its light, and the kings of the earth bring their glory and honor into it. Its gates shall not be shut at all by day (there shall be no night there). And they shall bring the glory and the honor of the nations into it."* The Kingdom of Heaven takes possession, extending the Heaven on Earth Experience to those who understand, respect, and walk in the Kingdom's Vision.

What if we are doing the right thing, and we are still clueless? The best way to Spiritually Align ourselves with our Purpose, Calling, Mission, or Talent is to begin a Mind Map Journal. The documentation of our thoughts, nudges, and instinctual messages will help guide us as long as we avail ourselves to the process without judgment.

In addition, we can also use this scripture to guide us. *"The Spirit of the Lord GOD is upon Me, because the LORD has anointed Me to preach good tidings to the poor; He has sent Me to heal the brokenhearted, to proclaim liberty to the captives, and the opening of the prison to those who are bound; to proclaim the acceptable year of the LORD, And the day of vengeance of our God; to comfort all who mourn, to console those who mourn in Zion, to give them beauty for ashes, the oil of joy for mourning, the garment of praise for the spirit of heaviness; that they may be called trees of righteousness, the planting of the LORD, that He may be glorified. And they shall rebuild the old ruins, they shall rise up the former desolations, and they shall repair the ruined cities, the desolations of many generations. Strangers shall stand and feed your flocks, and the sons of the foreigner shall be your plowmen and your vinedressers."* Isaiah 61:1-5.

After quoting Isaiah 61:1-5, then say, *'Speak Lord, your servant is listening.'* Write whatever comes to mind by documenting it in our Mind Map Journal. It does not have to be grammatically correct, and we do not have to understand it—the goal is to capture it on paper. After doing this for a period of 30 days, compare the instructions or notes from the first day to the current notes. One will notice an increase in alignment, then for another 30 days, repeat the same scripture, and add Psalm 45:1-2, *"My heart is overflowing with a good theme; I recite my composition concerning the King; my tongue is the pen of a ready writer. You are fairer than the sons of men; grace is poured upon your lips; therefore God has blessed you forever."* Continue this process until the unveiling, regrafting, or redirection occurs, leading toward the Kingdom of Heaven. Does it work? I will let you answer this question based on the journaling notes you are reading right now in this book, *Spiritual Calculations!* For indeed these are my *Spirit to Spirit* notes, *As It Pleased God.*

Royalty Rule Twenty-Three

The *Rules of Royalty* state that God wants us to build a solid foundation with Spiritual Principles, Concepts, Laws, and Precepts. What is the purpose of doing so? If our foundation is shaky or weak, then so are we. When building the foundation and erecting walls, we must use Heavenly Ingredients and Principles, along with the appropriate *Spiritual Calculations*, to ensure strength and levelness. God is very specific, precise, and well-calculated.

Here is how God is very instructional about the Kingdom, "*Now the wall of the city had twelve foundations, and on them were the names of the twelve apostles of the Lamb. And he who talked with me had a gold reed to measure the city, its gates, and its wall. The city is laid out as a square; its length is as great as its breadth. And he measured the city with the reed: twelve thousand furlongs. Its length, breadth, and height are equal. Then he measured its wall: one hundred and forty-four cubits, according to the measure of a man, that is, of an angel. The construction of its wall was of jasper; and the city was pure gold, like clear glass. The foundations of the wall of the city were adorned with all kinds of precious stones: the first foundation was jasper, the second sapphire, the third chalcedony, the fourth emerald, the fifth sardonyx, the sixth sardius, the seventh chrysolite, the eighth beryl, the ninth topaz, the tenth chrysoprase, the eleventh jacinth, and the twelfth amethyst.*" Revelation 21:14-20.

Why do we need to know this when it does not apply to us? Contrary to what most would assume, this scripture applies to us with a message hidden in plain sight.

The *Spiritual Calculations* of God do not deal with rubbish in the Kingdom! How can I say such a thing, especially when God says everything is good? Frankly, in the Book of Genesis, it is said before the fall of man; yet, after this point, we became tainted or impure, but still useable with the proper Spiritual Adornment.

Moreover, if we think for a minute that we can do whatever we want and think we can present it to the Kingdom in such fashion, we are sadly mistaken. We must clean up our act while stepping into the Spiritual Classroom for reformation and regrafting. Once again, we represent the Kingdom and not of ourselves; therefore, we must be presented according to the *Rules of Royalty* to secure its Secrets, Treasures, and Wisdom.

We cannot interject our perception into the Kingdom; we must avail ourselves to the Kingdom's Perception, *As It Pleases God*. He will not allow what is taking place here on Earth to penetrate His Kingdom, period.

Royalty Rule Twenty-Four

The *Rules of Royalty* state that God wants us to understand a few things regarding our Citizenship in the Heavenly of Heavens, but not limited to such:

- ☐ He wants us to understand 'Why' we were created and for 'Whom' to maximize the *Spiritual Calculations* of the Kingdom already grafted in our DNA.

- ☐ He wants us to understand that man's first fall in the 'Garden of Eden' was due to their disobedience. Their second fall in the same Garden was predicated on their pointing the finger (the blaming game) without assuming total responsibility for their behaviors, which *Cross-Contaminated* our Bloodline.

- ☐ He wants us to understand that the *Heavenly Sprinkles* of water will not cause a flood to wipe out everyone; it is designed to cleanse and baptize us individually.

- ☐ He wants us to understand that our *Heavenly Language* still exists.

- ☐ He wants us to understand that our *Spiritual Birthrights and Covenants* are still in full effect. We simply need to align ourselves with the Will of God, along with a willingness to use our Gifts, Calling, and Talents as He intended.

- ☐ He wants us to understand the *Value of Passover*, allowing nothing to separate us from the Blood of the Lamb, God, and our right to salvation.

- ☐ He wants us to understand our *Desert Experience* is designed to purify and develop our attitude toward Him, ourselves, and others.

- ☐ He wants us to understand our *Promised Land* is within our reach if we refuse to bicker, fuss, complain, and fight about the methods God uses to get us there.

- ☐ He wants us to understand that we are a *Chosen Generation*, and our lives are full of meaning, renewal, redemption, and freedom.

- ☐ He wants us to understand that our ability to read, document, and share our legacy will keep hope alive in those we have been ordained to inspire, mentor, or teach.

- ☐ He wants us to understand that the seed we are sowing today will bear fruit tomorrow; therefore, we should keep it on the positive side of the spectrum to maintain our Heavenly Insight or Vision.

- ☐ He wants us to understand that the Word of God is our roadmap of progression to keeping our lives on a straight and narrow Path of Greatness or Victory.

Why do we need all of the *Rules of Royalty* in the Kingdom? We are called upward to receive our double portion; therefore, we have rules governing the human psyche. Is this Biblical? *"I press toward the goal for the prize of the upward call of God in Christ Jesus. Therefore let us, as many as are mature, have this mind; and if in anything you think otherwise, God will reveal even this to you. Nevertheless, to the degree that we have already attained, let us walk by the same rule, let us be of the same mind. Brethren, join in following my example, and note those who so walk, as you have us for a pattern."* Philippians 3:14-17.

As we are called to higher heights, what about the double portion? Once the Rules of Royalty adequately govern us, here is what Isaiah 61:6-8 tells us: *"But you shall be named the priests of the LORD, they shall call you the servants of our God. You shall eat the riches of* the Gentiles, and in their glory you shall boast. Instead of your shame you shall have double honor, and instead of confusion they shall rejoice in their portion. Therefore in their land they shall possess double; everlasting joy shall be theirs. For I, the LORD, love justice; I hate robbery for burnt offering; I will direct their work in truth, and will make with them an everlasting covenant."

Chapter 12

Declarations of Revelation

The Declarations coming from the Kingdom of Heaven can give us Divine Revelation regarding its Treasures, Mysteries, and Secrets. How do we open Heaven's Gate on our behalf? We must learn how to truly apply the Word of God and His Principles to our everyday lives and not just put on a show one day a week.

When we are related in the Kingdom, we have more access than a foreigner. Still, suppose we do not possess a Kingdom Mentality, exhibiting the Fruits of the Spirit. In this case, we forfeit our rights to certain Treasures, Mysteries, and Secrets as well as Divine Revelation, even if we are faithfully serving God. Why does this seem like a slap in the face? According to the *Spiritual Calculations* of the Heavenly of Heavens, God is not looking for people to mimic Him. What does this mean? God is Absolute, and we are human with imperfections; therefore, the secret yearning we have from within for power is hidden under the word called dominion.

Unbeknown to most, the proper use of dominion takes place within the human psyche. How? Once again, the *'Garden of Eden'* is hidden within. To gain access to the Kingdom, we must become relatable, approachable, servantable, useable, and obedient while being open and willing to use our Gifts, Calling, and Talents toward our Divine Destiny, *As It Pleases Him.* Cluelessness leads to recklessness with or without our permission!

According to the *Spiritual Calculations* of the Heavenly of Heavens, we must know WHAT we are doing and WHY. We also need to become crystal clear about WHO we are in or out of the Kingdom.

What is the purpose of knowing this? It attracts the 'HOW-TO' from the Heavenly of Heavens like a magnet, or it will leave a trail of breadcrumbs to follow without becoming subjected to deception.

As it relates to the *Declarations of Revelation*, we are not here to serve ourselves, nor are we here to become selfish, stingy, disrespectful, or judgmental. We are here to serve others, and amid our Divine Commission, we become Blessed to be a Blessing. With this in mind, we can indeed uncomplicate our lives by becoming the Vessel God uses to accomplish His Purpose on Earth as it is in Heaven, which is the *Heaven on Earth Experience*.

How can we make it easier to usher in the presence of the Holy Spirit when we feel lost, blocked, or confused? Here is what can clear out the cobwebs, but not limited to such:

- ☐ Pray and repent of anything known or unknown, causing the aloofness.

- ☐ Become available by saying, 'Lord, I am available to walk in Your will and ways.'

- ☐ Usher in the Holy Spirit by requesting Him by saying, 'Holy Spirit, Your presence is needed, Come Forth in the Name of Jesus.'

- ☐ Open the relational dialogue by saying, 'Speak Lord, Your Servant is listening.'

- ☐ Make the *Declarations of Revelation* by saying, 'Open my eyes to see, open my ears to hear, and open my mouth to utter the Language of the Heavenly of Heavens.'

- ☐ Relax and wait, oxygenating our bodies. If we do not hear anything, we need to repeat the process. Why would we need to repeat the process? If we are in denial in the first step in the repenting portion, the Divine Connection can be withheld until we own our truth or take responsibility.

- [ ] Document, document, document. If we want relational dialogue from the Kingdom, we must capture it on paper. Once the *Declarations of Revelation* stop, we may not remember the instructions, information, or whatever; therefore, one must become an excellent note-taker. If not, one is not fit for Servanthood Revelation. As a result of our unpreparedness, we will receive inner chatter, distracting delusional images of untruths, and scattered thoughts instead. How can I say such a thing? Let me bring it down to reality. We would not go to class without taking notes, right? Of course not; we would fail. Case closed!

Failing in the Kingdom is not as bad as one would think. In fact, successes and failures in life make us better, giving us the experience needed to apply Heavenly Principles to reality. Furthermore, it also polishes our people skills and keeps us from judging others because we know how easy it is to fall short at the drop of a dime. The key to our *Declarations of Revelation* is knowing what to do when we fall short, what to say when others fall short, and how to listen to another man's story while asking the right questions to provoke healing or the element of thought.

In all reality, a Kingdom Mindset is comprised of being able to think, hear, and speak, *As It Pleases God*. All of the other hoopla is irrelevant. If we cannot think right, we become defeated. If we cannot hear correctly, we become defeated. If we cannot speak appropriately, we become defeated, regardless of our worldly accolades, credentials, or ego. Why is this so important? For example, personally, in a relationship, I need to know a few things. Just so we are clear, the list below is not judging; it is called paying attention:

- [ ] I need to know how a person thinks. If one is stuck on negative, they will attempt to draw me into the same web. If one thinks they are defeated mentally, they will try to convince me of the same. If one does not want to create a win-win out of a bad situation, they will count my wins as defeats. If one is worldly in their thinking, they will attempt to convince me that my *Heavenly Attempts* are of no earthly good.

- ☐ I need to know what a person is hearing, as well as how well they listen. If one cannot hear correctly, one will take what I say out of context without asking fact-finding questions to get an understanding. If one cannot listen, it is a Divine Revelation of disobedience, hidden rebellion, and selfishness. The bottom line is that if one develops a deaf ear to me, it is an automatic sign that they will develop a deaf ear to God and the Kingdom, especially when the conditions are shaky or uncontrollable.

- ☐ I need to know what a person is speaking about. What comes out of the mouth reveals the contents of our hearts, unveiling self-control or lawlessness. Also, I must know if one can speak life into me or whether they would annihilate me with their words. Now, as a word to the wise, if we listen long enough, people will tell us exactly what we need to know and how they would like to be treated, positively or negatively.

We can carry on with the charades of perfection, but according to the *Spiritual Calculations*, our fruits, senses, and character will give us a sum total of our present state of being, whether we agree or not.

The Divine *Declarations of Revelation* are all over the place, hidden in plain sight—we simply must understand the *Spiritual Calculations* associated. What does this mean? If we know what the Bible says about it, then we will recognize it once unveiled, but we must exhibit self-control. How? We do not need to respond to everything because the unveiling may be for our protection, self-awareness, or for us to tread with caution. More importantly, we must become Spiritually Astute to know precisely what to do or what not to do with the information, lessons, tests, and Blessings given.

Do great minds think alike? It depends on what we consider great. A controlled, worldly, or conditioned mind thinks like its master. With a Kingdom Mentality, the answer would be 'yes' due to the Oneness or the *Spiritual Calculations* of the Heavenly of Heavens. In my opinion, we must consider the perception of what we consider great as well, because Greatness in my eyes will not be such for another.

I am Spiritually Trained, Ordained, and Commissioned to see, hear, and speak what most cannot, which comes with the Levels of Spirituality from a Godly Perspective. Simply put, the *Spiritual Calculations* of the Heavenly of Heavens have Spiritually Unveiled the Laws, Principles, and Concepts of the Kingdom, giving me the ability to see through the Eye of God, which is available to all.

The positive thinkers and doers are the ones who benefit from a Kingdom Mentality. On the other hand, if we are negative, we will not recognize the benefits, even if they are right before our very eyes; we will find something wrong or a reason for it not being good enough. For example, someone can have a great relationship, yet they do not realize the value of it because their mind is locked in on something or someone better. As a result of the hidden or open ungratefulness, they will begin to complain, compare, and degrade their partner, putting willful rifts in the relationship as opposed to positively building it.

The ungoverned thoughts of better without gratefulness or when we intentionally create a negative in a positive situation due to ungoverned lusts or misinformation, we become susceptible to Spiritual Blinders, consuming all who fall into its grip. For this reason, we need to become thoroughly grateful for the good, bad, and ugly, even if we do not understand them at the time.

Without Spiritual Intervention, we do not know where the enemy has planted the seeds of deception, making us appear right in our own eyes. For this reason, we must always look for the Light and continuously work on ourselves from the inside out, exhibiting the Fruits of the Spirit and Christlike Character, becoming an example, as well as a Living Testimony to all.

What does the Light have to do with us? According to the *Spiritual Calculations* from the Heavenly of Heavens, "*The lamp of the body is the eye. If therefore your eye is good, your whole body will be full of Light. But if your eye is bad, your whole body will be full of darkness. If therefore the light that is in you is darkness, how great is that darkness!*" Matthew 6:22-23.

Why do we need to work on ourselves thoroughly to align ourselves with the Light? God does not need the 'Kingdom Gone-Bad Mentality' to bring about shame or make an absolute mess. He needs a 'Kingdom Get-It-Right Mentality' or the 'Work-In-Progress Mentality' to bring about Spiritual Illumination, making all things work together for our good. Besides, we also need to know this when dealing with the Light of the Kingdom: "*No one, having put his hand to the plow, and looking back, is fit for the Kingdom of God.*" Luke 9:62.

Once we get an understanding or we are crystal clear about the expectations from the Kingdom, we are better able to Spiritually Align ourselves in Earthen Vessels. For example, we are pursuing a person in hopes of developing a long-term relationship, yet the person on the opposite end does not have a clue about the relational plans or expectations. Therefore, they go about living their lives on their own terms, and then we have the nerve to get upset about them doing something we disagree with. But to add insult to injury, we secretly blame this person for cheating when a relationship and boundaries were never established in the first place.

The truth is that unclear or unfair expectations lead to them being unmet in some way, shape, or form due to our path of conveyance, the process of thought, conditioning, and biases. Meanwhile, in scripture, God is clear about the relationship He is expecting from us, and He does not make it a secret to see if we would err before committing. As a matter of fact, He is not waiting for us to become better or do better; He is all in with our flaws and all. More importantly, here is what He wants us to know: "*Blessed are those who are called to the marriage supper of the Lamb!"* Revelation 19:9.

When we manipulate the Kingdom's System to benefit ourselves, we are referred to as Scribes, Pharisees, or Hypocrites in Matthew 23. What is the purpose of name-calling? It is a label that unveils those who play by double standards while assuming a title without the Heavenly Fruits or Christlike Character to sustain the Kingdom Relationship. The Bible is also riddled with the label of adultery, adulterers, and adulteresses when we engage in negative monopolies and debauchery against the Kingdom, mainly when left unrepentant, uncorrected, or when we point the finger, degrading another as if we are perfect.

The bottom line is that we are all in this together, and if we expect something of someone, clarity is key. Even when it comes down to a Spiritual Relationship, we must become clear about our wants, desires, needs, or whatever. If we do not want to feel jilted, we must lay it on the table, allowing God to work it out. How can He work it out for us? He knows what is best for us and what is not.

What is the purpose of laying it on the table when God knows all? It is not about whether He knows. It is about whether we know the 'What,' understand our 'Why,' if we are true to ourselves, whether we are choosing to live a lie, or if we are going to become open to the 'How-To' process of our Divine *Declaration of Revelation*. Will God really do this for us? Absolutely, I am living proof.

To make an impact according to the *Spiritual Calculations* of the Heavenly of Heavens, we must begin by working on ourselves from the inside out. By doing so, it helps to spark the Creative Genius or Giant from within.

Once we uncover the debris blocking our Gifts, Callings, and Talents, we are better able to see the Light or redirect our focus to the positive, productive, and fruitful without falling prey to the negative. Allowing ourselves to recalculate or recalibrate on a moment-by-moment basis gives us the ability to think on our feet, in or out of season. In the simplicity of it all, we are able to go with the flow, even if we do not know what we are doing, as a part of the 'How-To' process.

The 'learn as we go' is a real and relevant privilege to those who pride themselves on possessing the Kingdom Mentality to break superficial limits, chains, yokes, or soul ties. Does it work for those out of the Kingdom? Yes, it does with a Positive Mental Mindset; however, there are limits as it relates to the Secrets, Mysteries, and Treasures of the Kingdom, as well as Divine Wisdom.

According to Spiritual Laws guarding the Kingdom of Heaven, we cannot extract where we have not sown or tread where we have not been trained to possess. What is the big deal? Spiritual Apprehension falls upon those who do not follow the Spiritual Protocol, *As It Pleases God*. Yet, the most elusive thing about it is that they will not know what is happening or what hit them until they repent or ask for Divine Revelation. Really? Yes, really!

There are certain things we cannot play around with, and the Kingdom of Heaven happens to be one of them. We can play church all day long, but when we tread into Kingdom Territory or when we are dealing with God's sheep, we must come correct. Just so we are clear, the wolf in sheep's clothing can play and tiptoe around looking for prey at his leisure, but he will get a rude awakening when he tries to circumvent the Mission of those possessing Kingdom Credentials or the Mark of the Kingdom. God owns everything, including the wolf. And, being that God is the Head Chief in charge, He will shut everything or everyone down to restore his sheep or place them in a fold when they repentantly cry out for help, period.

When it comes down to the Principles of the Kingdom, we cry out to God, but we forget to repent. Then we have the nerve to blame God for not answering us or remaining silent amid our amissness. Really? Yes, really. We do not need to be well-versed in Kingdom Principles to use them according to the way Jesus simply laid them out for us. What does this mean? The Lord's Prayer gives us a bird's-eye view of Kingdom Expectations.

If we omit repentance or forgiveness amid our prayers, we sell our souls short. How? We become a target of deception with the 'Anything goes' or 'I will do it myself' Mentality. What does deception have to do with forgiveness or repentance? Deception is a derivative of residing in unforgiveness or the lack of repentance of the impurities lurking from within. Also, it prevents the Holy Spirit from residing within us as we knowingly or unknowingly give way to the dark side, our self-aggrandizing ways of selfishness, or outright worldliness. More importantly, if we are not repenting, it is evident that we are not forgiving God, ourselves, something, or someone.

Unbeknown to most, repenting and forgiving, or the lack of them, are intertwined in ways beyond human comprehension. Is this Biblical? Here is the Divine *Declaration of Revelation*, *"For if you forgive men their trespasses, your heavenly Father will also forgive you. But if you do not forgive men their trespasses, neither will your Father forgive your trespasses."* Matthew 6:14-15.

What can we do to Spiritually Seal our prayers to become Spiritual Ammunition? Jesus provided the answer in the Lord's Prayer: *"In this manner, therefore, pray: Our Father in Heaven, Hallowed be Your name. Your Kingdom come. Your will be done on earth as it is in Heaven. Give us this day our daily bread. And forgive us our debts, as we forgive our debtors. And do not lead us into temptation, but deliver us from the evil one. For Yours is the kingdom and the power and the glory forever. Amen."* Matthew 6:9-13.

If we do our job to repent and forgive, God will do His. What is His job? To take care of us as His sheep, granting us the Benefits of the Kingdom while in or out of the Spiritual Classroom, regardless of what Spiritual Level we are on. In addition, we have the Blood of Jesus to cover us, and we have the Holy Spirit to help us convert negatives into positives, create a win-win out of everything, and help us become grateful regardless of how it may appear to the natural eye.

When we bond with God and His Kingdom, we position ourselves to step into our rightful Birthright to reveal the Light of the Heavenly of Heavens. Yet, we also have those who are okay with exposing some Light without becoming the Light as well. What is the difference? One becomes the Earthen Vessel being used for the Kingdom to provide Divine Illumination, *As It Pleases God*. The other shares the Light without becoming it, or they shift the responsibility to another, declining to become or live by example to please themselves.

The Examples of the Kingdom have been set before us in plain sight as our *Declaration of Revelation*. But for some odd reason, we have missed the value in the examples of who we are and why, according to the Divine Will of God. How are we missing the mark? It is through our inability to operate in our Servanthood abilities with Kingdom Servitude. At the same time, we are fighting about who is right and who is wrong as it relates to Religion.

We are free to serve, and we are born to serve. Now, suppose we do not understand this fact. In this case, we will begin to fight against each other for dominion for the dominatory placement of what we perceive as being right in our own eyes, for the sake of Religion. Due to this preclusive oversight, we become oblivious to the value of establishing and maintaining a Kingdom Relationship or having a Heaven on Earth Experience.

The Bible is not a book of bondage, war, hate, or privilege of a certain type of denomination. Even though there are gruesome stories containing such behaviors, they also reveal consequences to help us in such a time as this, revamping our perspective from back then and right now. According to the *Spiritual Calculations* of the Heavenly of Heavens, the Bible is to be used as a Book of Freedom, a Book of Examples, a Book of Love, and a Book of Guidance for all who are willing to embrace the Divine Wisdom, Treasures, Revelations, and Mysteries it holds.

As a Vessel of the Kingdom, we are required to become an example for those we are leading, as well as the ones sitting on the sidelines, spectating. With or without our permission, people are watching us to determine if the Kingdom is what we proclaim it to be or to cast a little shade. This is why we must bring the Light to the table at all times, even if we make a mistake.

The Spiritual Transparency comprised in our Humble Servitude deflects the shadowy intents of those who are designed to discredit the Kingdom or steal our shine. Humbly repenting in a mess up to create a win-win for the Kingdom makes us better, stronger, and more Spiritually Astute to flip the script on the enemy, reclaiming our Light. How? The moment the enemy thinks he is taking us down, we are strategizing for our come-up or come-back by becoming a Spiritual Servant to the Kingdom. Here is what Jesus had to say about this: *"If I then, your Lord and Teacher, have washed your feet, you also ought to wash one another's feet. For I have given you an example, that you should do as I have done to you. Most assuredly, I say to you, a Servant is not greater than His master; nor is he who is sent greater than He who sent him. If you know these things, blessed are you if you do them."* John 13:14-17.

According to the *Spiritual Calculations* of the Heavenly of Heavens, by using this one Spiritual Servanthood Principle, the enemy has limited access to those who have both feet in the Kingdom. By far, when working as a Spiritual Vessel, leading God's sheep to greener pastures with clean hands and a pure heart with the Fruits of the Spirit in hand while exhibiting Christlike Character, God will protect what belongs to Him, period. And if He allows the enemy to tempt, try, or pounce on us, it **must** become a Blessing, a footstool, or recompense must be rendered at some point before it is all said and done. If one does not know this, they will become dead-set on leading themselves in worldliness, unforgiveness, hatefulness, debauchery, jealousy, envy, greed, covetousness, payback, and the list goes on with negative attributes.

How can we enable the Kingdom to work on our behalf? According to scripture: *"Likewise, exhort the young men to be sober-minded, in all things showing yourself to be a pattern of good works; in doctrine showing integrity, reverence, incorruptibility, sound speech that cannot be condemned, that one who is an opponent may be ashamed, having nothing evil to say of you. Exhort bondservants to be obedient to their own masters, to be well pleasing in all things, not answering back, not pilfering, but showing all good fidelity, that they may adorn the doctrine of God our Savior in all things."* Titus 2:6-10. Once done, *"After these things I heard a loud voice of a great multitude in heaven, saying, Hallelujah! Salvation and glory and honor and power belong to the Lord our God!"* Revelation 19:1.

The Kingdom is already ours; it is our Divine Birthright. All it takes is for us to believe in ourselves, and we can claim what is rightfully ours while gaining the Spiritual Credentials to take our rightful possession, *As It Pleases God*.

Why wait any longer? The Journey is NOW! *"He who overcomes shall be clothed in white garments, and I will not blot out his name from the Book of Life; but I will confess his name before My Father and before His angels. He who has an ear, let him hear what the Spirit says to the churches."* Revelation 3:5-6.

For I am my brother's keeper, from me to you, this is the Call of the Kingdom, will you answer? Remember, according to the *Spiritual Calculations* and the *Declarations of Revelation* from the Heavenly of Heavens, *Royalty* is in your Blood. And whatever you need is already.

In conclusion, believing in yourself is vital to achieving success and living a fulfilled life, *As It Pleases God*. May your path be Divinely Illuminated with countless BLESSINGS because I believe in you. Until we meet again, joined in the REALM of Spirit and Truth, GROW GREAT!

Dr. Y. Bur

www.ingramcontent.com/pod-product-compliance
Lightning Source LLC
Chambersburg PA
CBHW071622170426
43195CB00038B/1875